The Dress you Wear and how to Make It

The Dress You Wear

and

How to Make It

By

Mary Jane Rhoe

Illustrated

G. P. Putnam's Sons
New York and London
The Knickerbocker Press
1918

The Knickerbocker Press, New York

THERE is no question in my mind about this text being a very practical and helpful one. The author tested out every one of its lessons in our class rooms before deciding to publish them in book form. She is not offering, therefore, theories and unused plans, merely hoping that everything will work out all right.

There is certainly a need for such a book as Mrs. Rhoe's. Oral instruction in dressmaking and plain sewing is not sufficient where one desires the best possible results. The student needs to listen to the oral instruction given by the teacher, but she learns her sewing problems quicker and better if she has the opportunity when alone to read and re-read her teacher's printed directions and explanations.

The matter in the book is presented so simply that our evening school students had no trouble in understanding its directions.

This statement means much when we consider that many evening school students are adults who do not have the opportunity to complete even the eighth grade when in school. The simple presentation causes no lack of interest, however, on the part of the more advanced student. The text appeals strongly to all who use it. These are not guesses and predictions. Our knowledge in this case is born of experience.

FRANK H. ARNOLD
Principal Lewis & Clark Evening School
Spokane, Washington

PREFACE

This book is intended to present the principal and important details of dressmaking. It offers a concise system for use in evening and vocational schools, which are now so thoroughly established, so that students may receive in their study hours the very essence of the art. The author has endeavored to make the lessons so plain, so practical, and so condensed that the young girl as well as the woman of mature years may advance rapidly.

It will solve problems for the home dressmaker and the busy *Madame* in her shop.

Dressmaking is one of the most interesting studies, also one of the most important that we have to-day.

We should be individual in our dress, yet there are rules set by Dame Fashion to which we must conform in order to be modern; this requires a thorough knowledge of the art.

The consciousness of an appropriate and becoming costume develops ease of manner. On the other hand, poorly fitted and imperfectly made clothes or cheap shoddy garments cause embarrassment and self-consciousness.

Over-dress is always bad taste.

The knowledge of dress for different occasions is, therefore, not only valuable but *necessary* to every woman, and it is the hope of the author that this small volume, the result of much experience, will prove of true value and assistance to its readers.

M. J. R.

SPOKANE, 1918.

SUGGESTIONS TO TEACHERS

It is not necessary to follow to the letter the order of teaching as given here, but we have found it desirable to produce a system for the advanced class in dressmaking by which students can be given examinations and receive credits as in other school work.

This is an incentive to faithful and continued attendance to reach a required standard of efficiency.

It has been arranged for the evening class by giving the first half of the last period to class work. The change at this time rests and relieves those not used to the work.

Recitations, written or oral, and samplers made of all the different stitches, pockets, covering cord for ornamental purposes, shirring on cord, flat shirring, tucked shirring, smocking, buttonholes, eyelets, loops, etc.

The following lesson to be given should be

assigned and discussed with students to give an opportunity for home study.

Give as much time to class work as can be managed, as a large class can be handled with more satisfaction to teacher and student after these details are understood by the class.

CONTENTS

CHAPTER I

CHAPTER II

The Dress You Wear

The Dress You Wear

CHAPTER I

Nap

ALL wool materials with nap should be cut so that the nap runs down.

All silk materials with nap, such as velvet and plushes, with the exception of panne velvet should be cut so the nap runs up. In panne velvets, the nap runs down.

If cut so that the nap of one piece of the material runs up and another piece runs down the effect is a light and a dark shade.

Velvets and plushes should be brushed so the nap stands out.

To determine which way the nap runs, lay material right side up on work table, with the hand brush the material lengthwise to the right, then to the left. When brushing against the nap the material will feel rough, and when brushing with the nap the material is smooth.

Right Side of Material

To determine the right side of goods in serge or diagonal weaves, the twill runs to the right on the right side of material. The right side in double-fold material is usually folded inside. This is done to protect the right side from becoming shelf worn or soiled by handling while in the store.

Another good test is to hold the cloth up to the light and look across it, the wrong side will have a rough look, and usually some unfinished ends or small knots are to be seen.

Suitable Material for Extreme Figures

Tall, slender figures may wear plaids, figured or plain materials, also designs that tend to shorten the figure, such as numerous flounces, ruffles, overskirts, etc., while short, stout figures should wear stripes, small checks, and plain materials made in designs to bring out the full height.

It is also important to select colors becoming to the individual regardless of the prevailing style.

Selection of Material for Gowns and Suits

Soft, light-weight materials are required for fancy-draped gowns, heavy materials for tailored dresses and suits.

Shrinking

It is absolutely necessary that goods be shrunken and sponged before being made up. First, procure a piece of heavy, unbleached muslin a yard wide and one-half yard longer than the material, wring muslin out as dry as possible after dipping in warm water, lay smoothly on table, placing material on top, leaving it folded through the center so right sides face each other. Leave muslin one-half yard to fold over material covering first roll. Leave in roll two to four hours, unroll, and press thoroughly dry on wrong side of goods.

Taking Measures

Neck measure should be taken at base or lower part of neck. Bust measure close up under the arms over full part of back and about one inch above the full part of bust. This measure is to be easy. Waist measure, draw tape tight around the waist.

Front, from lower part of tape around the neck to center of tape at waistline.

Chest measure in line with highest outer point of shoulder, half-way between shoulder and full part of bust. Have this measure as wide as can be worn.

Width of back, take measure as in chest, half-way between top of shoulder and bust line, also as wide as can be worn.

Underarm, from waistline well up under the arm.

Sleeve measurements, length of sleeve outside over elbow with elbow bent.

Inside length, with arm in natural position hanging down.

Hand measure, around largest part of hand over thumb.

Skirt measure, around the hips seven inches from waistline, not tight, but easy.

Front, from waistline to floor.

Side, from waistline over fullest part of hips to floor.

Back, from waistline to floor and not too close to figure.

Altering and Testing Patterns

Become familiar with the pattern before using it.

Measure from neck line in front to perfora-

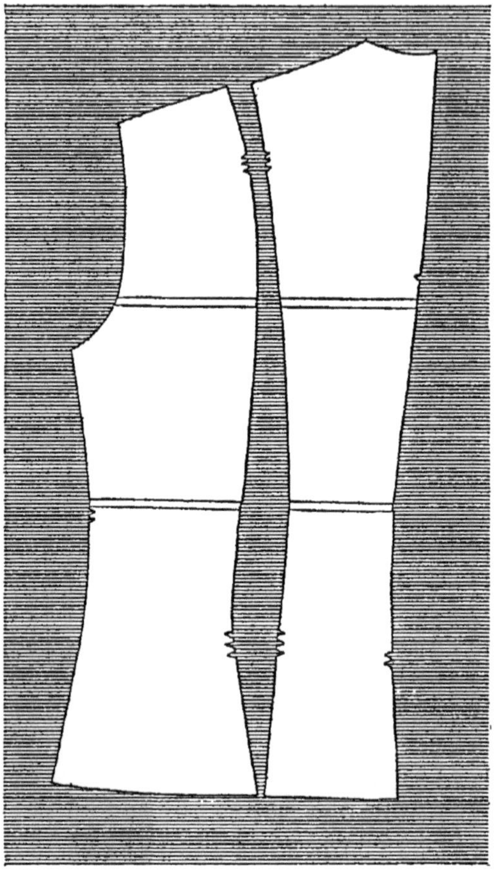

TO LENGTHEN WAIST PATTERN

tions for waistline, allowing two or three inches for blouse if desired.

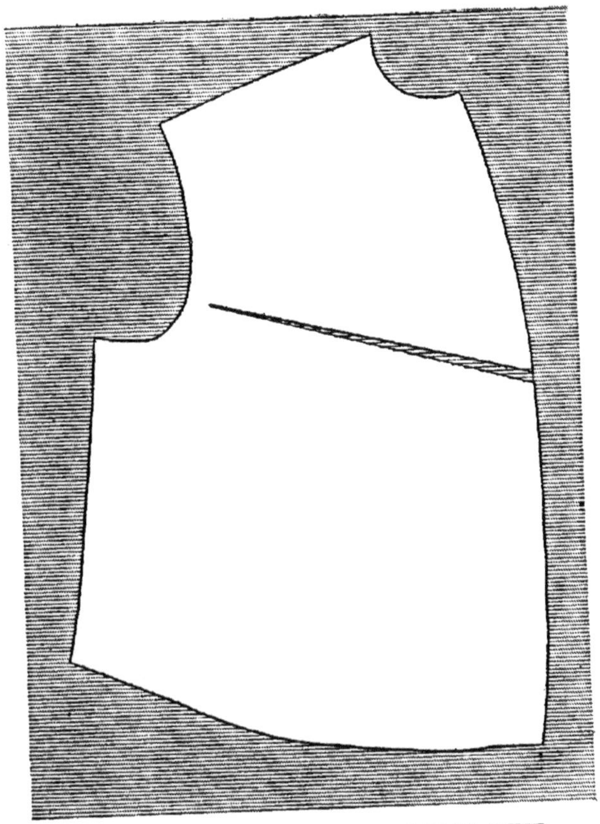

ALTERATION FOR EXTREME LARGE BUST

Measure underarm from lowest part of armhole to waistline perforations.

In shirtwaist and in shirtwaist effects

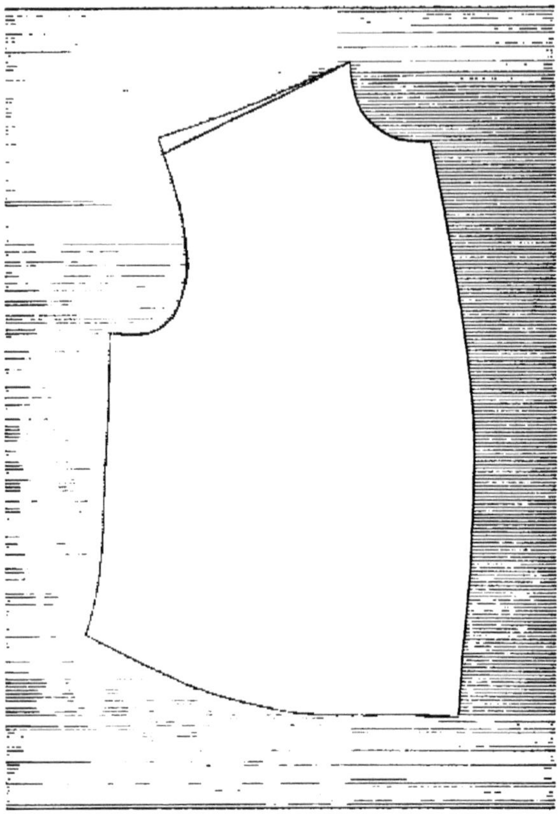

ALTERATION FOR SLOPING SHOULDERS

always leave waistline longer than in one-piece dresses, with belt or high waistline, also two inches larger at bust than measure taken.

ALTERATION FOR SQUARE SHOULDERS

Test chest and shoulder widths, especially for round shoulders, and if necessary cut a little wider across shoulders.

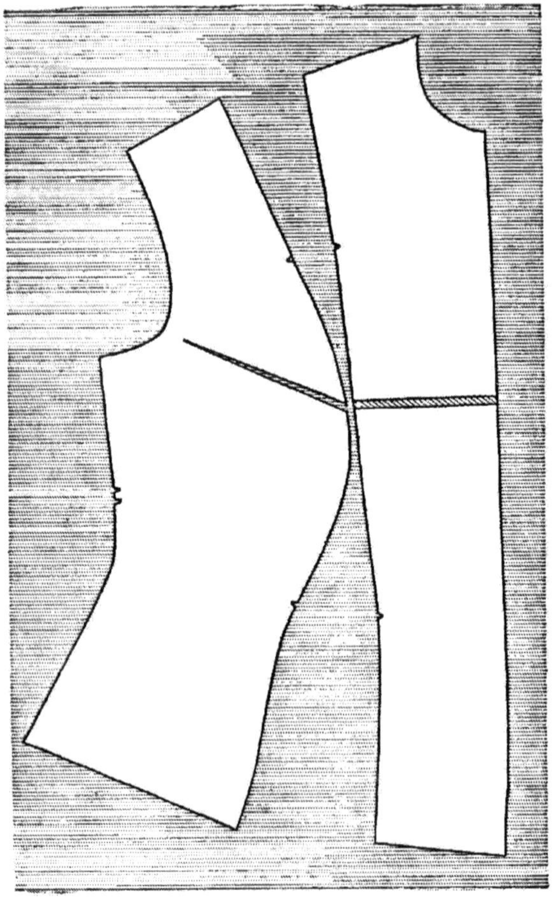

ALTERATION FOR EXTREME FULL BUST

If pattern proves too long lay in a fold half-way between waistline and armhole

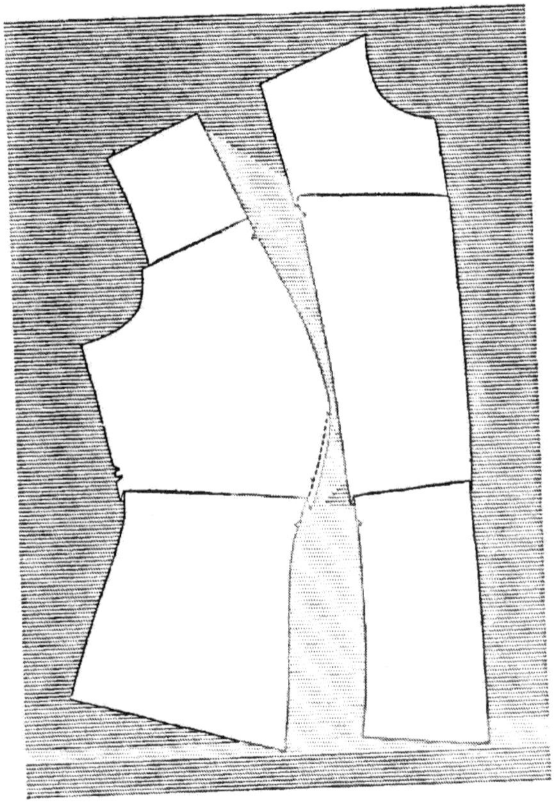

TO SHORTEN WAIST OF PATTERN

deep enough to relieve the unnecessary length.

For extremely full bust, especially in Princess dresses, slash pattern across bust within

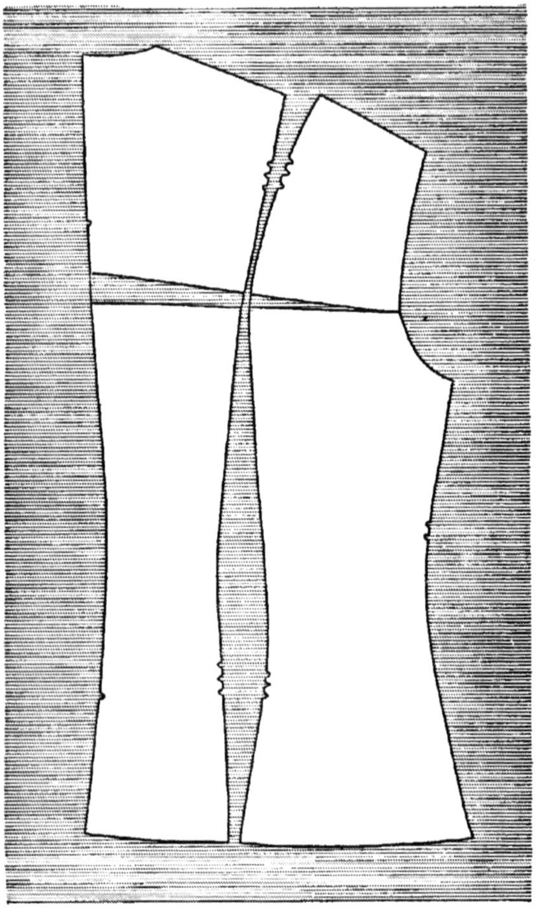

ALTERATION FOR FULL ROUND SHOULDERS

one and one-half inches of armhole (this

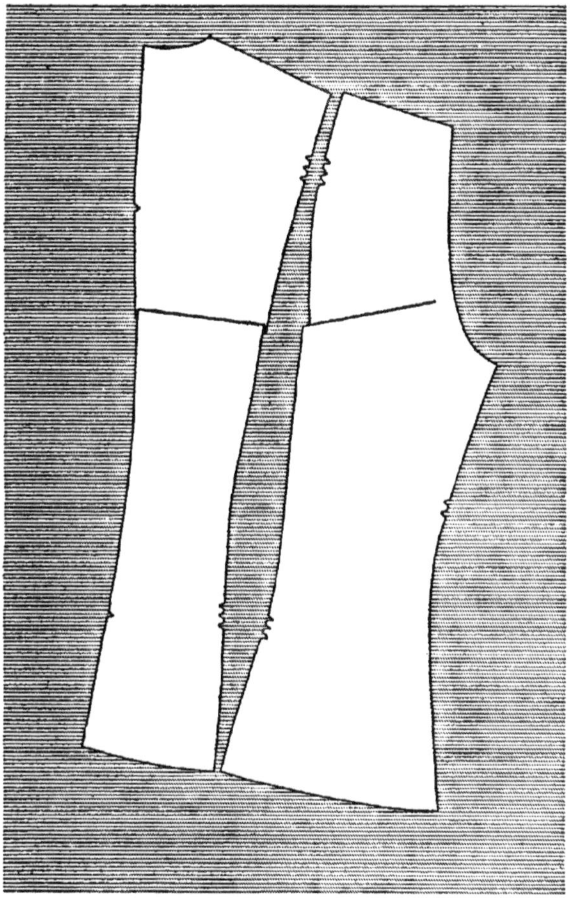

ALTERATION FOR EXTREME SMALL BUST AND FLAT SHOULDERS

should be done after pattern is pinned up

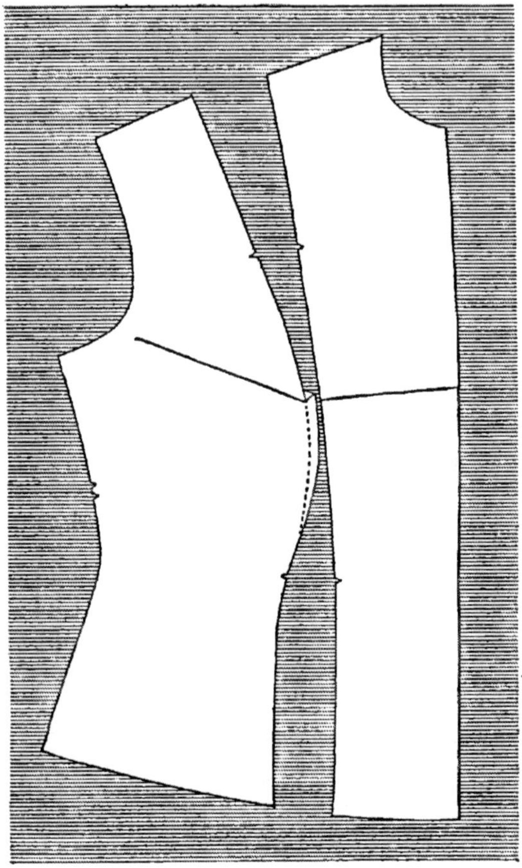

ALTERATION FOR EXTREME SMALL BUST AND FLAT SHOULDERS

and tried on the figure). Adjust pattern to

waistline correctly which will leave open space at bust. Slip under the edges of slash, another piece of paper, pin to pattern on both edges of slash to give necessary room for bust.

This same alteration is sometimes necessary in the back in case of round shoulders.

This alteration also prevents a draw under the arm caused by the large bust lifting the garment in front.

In case of extremely small bust or flat shoulders take a fold in pattern to fit figure.

Alteration of Sleeve Pattern

The most common difficulty is the sleeve that pulls on the back seam from the elbow up and frequently under the arms, strongly enough to tear the sleeve from the armhole before the garment is half worn out. In this case the sleeve is too short from the elbow up, causing this pull when the elbow is used.

Test pattern by pinning up and trying on

of sleeve pinned in pattern for the dress, then place the hand on the opposite shoulder and if this is easily done the sleeve is correct. If there is a pull from shoulder to elbow, cut upper part longer than pattern. If too long from elbow to shoulder in this position when elbow of sleeve is also in proper position lay fold in pattern sufficient to take out unnecessary length.

Sleeve may be shortened or lengthened below the elbow, but first be sure that the elbow of pattern is in correct position on the arm.

In pinning sleeve into armhole the highest point in sleeve top should be placed at highest point in armhole at shoulder, and lowest point at underarm at lowest point in armhole.

Alteration of Skirt Pattern

Many of our skirt patterns are cut for high waistline which allows from two and one-half to three inches above the waist.

The normal waistline is always marked in the front gore usually by two small perforations.

Take measure as previously instructed from normal waistline which is located by tying a narrow tape around the waist snug. It naturally adjusts itself to the smallest part of waist which is the proper waistline.

Measure from waistline to floor in front, also over full part of hip and back (allowing tape to be farther from figure in back than sides and front) and always take measure to floor.

Take from this measure the number of inches from the floor you wish your skirt to be, allowing for depth of hem in bottom of skirt, if it is to be hemmed. If only a little too long the bottom of the pattern may be turned up two inches, but if more is required put a fold through the center of the pattern, remember the fold takes out twice its width like a tuck. If pattern is too short lengthen at the bottom.

After pinning on material for cutting, use skirt rule and lay rule alongside edge of pattern, allowing it to extend the required number of inches and mark both edges of pattern from end of pattern down to end of extra length while in position. This gives you the correct line for the additional length.

Measure from lower edge of pattern the required number of inches to make long enough all around, mark every three or four inches with tailors' chalk, draw a line connecting these marks. This gives you the correct length, also keeping the circular shape of skirt at the bottom.

Measure around full part of hips seven inches below waistline. This measure should be easy like bust measure. A skirt is never graceful if too tight around the hips.

Measure skirt pattern around hips, leaving it amply large as it is easy to fit in a little, but if too small it is not easily altered.

If skirt proves much too large a tiny fold may be taken in center of pattern, again remembering the fold takes out twice its width and, as you are always using one-half of pattern, the same amount will come out of the opposite gore for the other side of skirt.

If your pattern is too small around divide the amount in half, then divide the half into as many parts as you have gores, adding to each gore the required amount to make correct size. For example: A skirt of seven gores would have three gores on each side and the front gore with seam in center back. Therefore, if skirt was seven inches too small there would be one inch to add to each gore in width adding one-half inch on each side of pattern. This is given as an example of extreme case to make the alteration plain.

In adding to or taking from the width of pattern make the same alteration the full length of pattern to keep the outline and shape of skirt correct. Any other alterations should be made in the fitting of the garment.

If length of back and hip seem too long

after skirt is correct by front measure, it should be lifted a little at the back when skirt is fitted and a little taken from the top in back. This will prevent a flat look in the back and also a pouching out at the bottom in front.

Questions

1. How should the nap of the material run on woolen material?

2. How should the nap of the material run on silk materials such as velvet and plushes?

3. How should the nap of the material run on panne velvet?

4. Give suggestions as to finding right side of materials.

5. What materials would you suggest suitable for tall, slender figures?

6. What care should be taken in selecting colors?

7. What materials are suitable for fancy-draped gowns? What for tailored gowns and suits?

8. How do we prepare material before cutting?

9. Describe method of shrinking cloth.

10. Where should the neck measure be taken? Bust? Waist? Front? Chest? Width of back? Underarm?

11. What two sleeve measures should be taken? Where is the hand measure taken?

12. What is the first step required in studying a pattern?

13. About what difference is there between the normal and high waistline?

14. Describe how to test the entire pattern.

15. How should you change a pattern for full bust? For round shoulders? For flat bust? For flat shoulders?

16. What causes a sleeve to pull on the back seam from the elbow up?

17. How would you test a sleeve pattern?

18. Describe how to pin a sleeve in the armhole.

19. How do we take skirt measures?

20. How would you shorten a skirt pattern?

21. How would you lengthen a skirt pattern?

22. How would you make a pattern smaller around hips? How larger?

23. Give example of enlarging a seven-gored skirt.

24. Is it necessary to make alterations full length of skirt?

25. How would you correct a skirt if length of back and hips are too long?

CHAPTER II

Equipment

It is as necessary that a home dressmaker has the proper tools to work with as a carpenter.

Without them one is handicapped in various ways and is liable to find the work a discouraging task.

In these days of advancement and progress, even the Home woman is learning that there is a limit to endurance, and home life and duties should be made a pleasure and all work done in a business-like way.

This, one of the home studies and economic feature of the housewife's accomplishments, sewing, has been much of a task because of lack of knowledge on the subject, also lack of equipment.

This sewing work-shop is as necessary to

the worker as the kitchen is to the cook. Surgeons, doctors, and nurses make equipment the first consideration. Yet we take a pair of old dull shears and cut uneven edges in good material and get along as best we can, which is all wrong.

Let us have everything necessary to turn out good work in our home dressmaking parlors, so that our work will not look home-made.

Dress form.
Skirt guage.
Shears (9 or 10 inches long).
Paper of needles (No. 7).
Basting cotton (No. 60).
Skirt rule 48 inches long, bought at a tailors' supply house.
Tape line.
Pins, with good points.
Emery bag.
Tracing wheel.
Tailors' chalk.
Beeswax.

Tailors' punch, bought at hardware store or tailors' supply house (for buttonholes).

Tailors' cushions (2 sizes).

Press cloth.

Sponge.

Whisk broom.

Two pressing irons (12 pounds and 6 pounds).

Sewing table.

Sewing machine.

Sewing room to be light and airy.

Dress Form

To make a dress form satisfactory, one that is in form and figure like yourself, one that you can really put your dress on and see the lines and general effect just as you look, is not expensive. You only need to buy a cheap form and need not pay over four dollars and fifty cents or five dollars for same.

It should be at least one size smaller than your own bust measure for this reason: Your form and this form will not be just alike (the bust on a dress form is usually large).

A lining should be made of drilling or some material that will not stretch. The lining should be as long as the body of the form and should be cut in at least six sections and fitted very snug. If it wrinkles at waistline over hips make a small crosswise fold extending just far enough and just deep enough to take out wrinkles and stitch flat. It should fit like a glove. Pad form wherever necessary with wadding, such as tailors use in coats, to make it fit smooth and be like your own natural form.

This will require time and a careful adjustment and re-adjusting as you will not get it correct by just putting wadding on until lining is filled out.

If hips are rather large, fill them out; if abdomen is large, fill out; if shoulders are round, fill out.

This form can be made a complete duplicate of yourself when finished. Then, in making a gown, you may be able to see the effect and where change in line or style would be especially beneficial to your figure.

Skirts may be hung and length taken when you have form finished. Measure bust, hips, etc., and compare with your measures. Put a small tape around waist to get correct waistline the same as to get correct waistline on yourself. Leave the tape there for future use in fitting, etc.

Pinning Seams before Basting

All seams should be pinned before basting to avoid having one side fulled in the basting. Without pinning, the side of the seam held toward you will ease in and cause trouble. When fitting in waists and coats pin waistline first, then pin from waistline to shoulder and from waistline to bottom of garment. In skirts lay both edges to be basted smoothly on work table, edges even. While in this position pin edges about three inches apart, placing pins, the heads toward the outer edge of seams, the points into materials.

If this is carefully done before basting and the stitching is straight, a careful pressing will complete a perfect seam. The seam should look as straight as if glued.

Material Required for a Garment

First, the design should be carefully considered which should be controlled by what we need this special garment for. Whether for street, special dress, or for all around wear. Then, the money we can afford to put in it, is another consideration.

Never dress beyond your means. If carefully planned and bought one's wardrobe need not cost so much.

To be economical do not buy conspicuous material or use extreme styles.

One or two garments a year of good material and well made means better dressed than five or six cheap half-made affairs.

When you have decided what your design is to be procure your pattern, read all the instructions, pin pattern up, try it on and make necessary alterations.

Select material but do not buy until you find out just how much you will need, then you will neither buy too much nor too little. Although it is wise to buy a little more than enough and have some left to alter your dress later on.

To determine how much material is needed measure a space on the floor or work table with chalk the width of material you are to use, then place all pieces of pattern on this. Be sure to notice if the material has a nap to lay pattern on so nap runs all one way, as we have already learned the importance of, in a previous lesson, then buy material. Have it shrunken or shrink it yourself as taught in previous lesson.

In wool goods never pay any attention to the salesman who says it has been sponged and shrunken, as you are liable to meet with much trouble by so doing.

A tailor always shrinks his material no matter what any one says. Now you are ready to proceed with cutting and making your garment. Never rush.

A student of a fine, high-class tailor in New York, where no suit or dress was made in his establishment for less than one hundred dollars, was trying to hurry. She was little more than a child and this had been her ambition; to make beautiful tailored gowns and suits. She had often looked in the windows and watched the tailors work and how fast their hands flew, and of course she thought she must do the same. But the kind-faced old tailor saw how nervously she was trying to hurry and realized what a mistake she was making. He came to her and said: "Little lady, we try here to see how well our work can be done; not how much we can do."

Be master of your work, sure of yourself first, then practice speed.

The beauty of the garment, whether material is expensive or cheap, is in the construction.

Fitting a Skirt

When a skirt is ready to fit, pin center of front and center of back where they belong on the person.

If gored skirt see that seams are straight from hip line to waistline. If too large pin in seams, be careful to pin the seams on both sides and the same seams.

If one hip is larger than the other, noticeably so, pad the small hip a little so the person will not look crooked. Pin in padding while skirt is being fitted. A skirt should always fit easily enough to be eased slightly into the band or belting, it will hang much more gracefully.

If person is very slender it is sometimes necessary to lift skirt in back and slightly to the sides to prevent the skirt from swinging front and pouching out or having a saggy look in the back. Remove skirt, make all necessary changes, pin and baste to band or belting, and try on again.

If correct the length may be taken. Never try to get the length until the fitting is complete and skirt to position on band.

Questions

1. In home dressmaking is it necessary to have proper equipment?

2. In what way does the proper equipment assist?

3. Name the articles required in the home dressmaking equipment.

4. What kind of a dress form would you suggest buying?

5. Explain how to pad a dress form to fit the person.

6. If the fitted cover wrinkles at the hip, what is the remedy?

7. How do you mark the waistline?

8. Is it necessary to pin seams before basting?

9. In fitting waists and coats where should you begin to pin?

10. Describe how to pin a skirt.

11. In selecting material what should be considered?

12. Would you prefer one or two good garments to many gaudy ones?

13. Is conspicuous material economical?

14. How can you determine the amount of material needed?

15. Is it necessary to shrink goods?

16. Describe how to fit a skirt.

CHAPTER III

Basting

ALL seams should be carefully pinned before basting (see subject for pinning).

Long seams in skirts should be basted flat

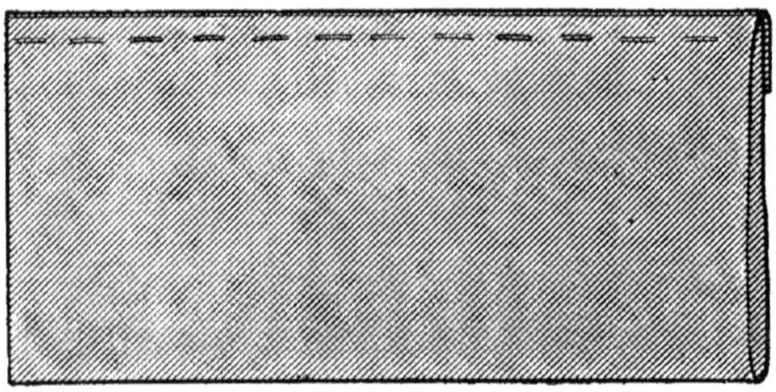

BASTING

on table, the same as for pinning. If you prefer to hold material while basting, keep it straight. Do not hold it over the finger or curve it in any way as by so doing the curved side held towards you will be eased in, even after a careful pinning, and when finished the seam will look as if one side was gathered.

In princess dresses, long semi-fitted coats, basques, and tight linings, after pinning as taught in article on pinning, baste from waistline up and from waistline down, and the garment will not twist as it is liable to do otherwise. Do not take stitches too long and never pull basting too tight, as it has a tendency to draw the whole seam.

To Prevent Twisting of Two-Piece Sleeve

In basting a two-piece or coat sleeve, baste inside seam first, then lay on work table with upper or larger section underneath—smooth out flat. About three inches from top, fold the upper section over to the under part of sleeve just where it comes naturally and pin; also about three inches from the bottom fold and pin. Continue pinning from both ends of sleeve to within two and one-half inches of elbow, gather whatever fullness comes in that space on the upper side of sleeve; adjust the gathers, pin, and baste. Then lay sleeve flat on table in same position and if it draws or will not stay in correct shape you have not made the first joining correct.

Pay no attention to whether the ends come out even in top or bottom of sleeve, but join back section to under section so as to leave upper and under of sleeve lie flat and smooth while pinning in place, then the sleeve will not twist.

Basting Velvets and Silks

Cotton thread leaves a mark when used in basting silks and velvets, therefore, you should use silk thread. Clip bastings every four or five inches, sometimes closer, as pulling a long basting in fine sheer material, especially silks, is liable to tear the goods or make a bad mark.

Bias or Diagonal Basting

This is used to baste the outside and lining together where the lining is eased in, leaving the outside a little tighter than the lining.

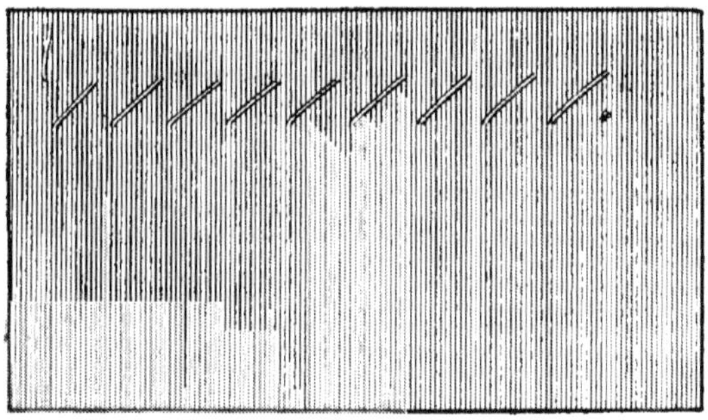

BIAS OR DIAGONAL BASTING

The stitches are from three-fourths of an inch to one and one-half inches long and from one inch to two inches apart. Take stitches toward you and usually crosswise of goods which leaves a diagonal thread between the stitches. The stitches may be longer or shorter, according to material used and necessity of it being held firmly to lining while the finish of the garment is in progress.

Padding Stitch

This stitch is used by tailors on lapels and coat collars. It is the same as diagonal or bias basting only the stitch is not more than one-half inch long and one-half inch apart.

The work is done on the canvas side of the garment and barely catching the material of the right side.

Running Stitch

A running stitch is made by taking even-length, small stitches. With careful prac-

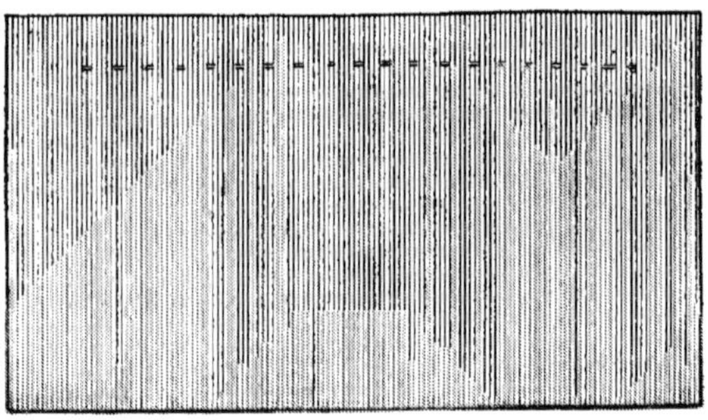

RUNNING STITCH

tice it can be done rapidly from which it derives its name. Keep edges of seam even by pinning (see subject of pinning), sew an even, straight seam putting needle in and out of material, making space and stitch of even length.

Back Stitch

In the back stitch, the under stitch is twice the length of the upper stitch. Bring needle

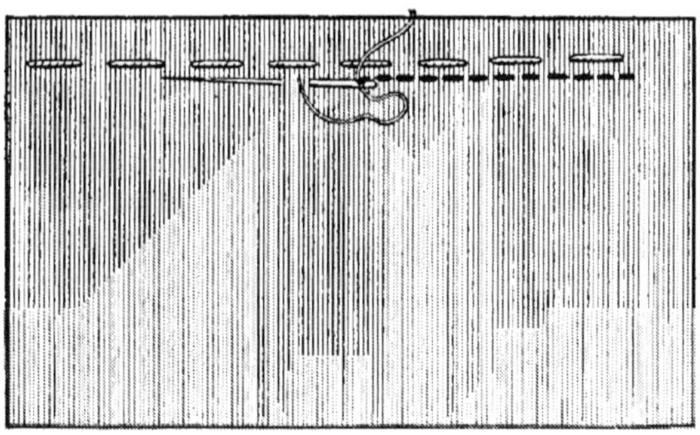

BACK STITCH

up through material a stitch ahead, then set needle one-half length of the under stitch back of where the under stitch came out, then again bring needle up through material one stitch ahead and set needle for second stitch back to meet the first upper stitch. This stitch is used where a strong seam is required.

Combination Stitch

This is used in sewing by hand where a firm running stitch is not strong enough and every third or fourth of your running stitch is a back stitch.

Questions

1. What should be done before basting?
2. How should you baste long seams in a skirt?
3. Where should you begin pinning the seams in princess dresses, long semi-fitted coats, and tight linings?
4. Should basting be pulled tight?
5. Describe how to baste a two-piece sleeve.
6. What kind of thread should be used in basting silk or velvet?
7. Describe the padding stitch.
8. For what is bias basting used?
9. How did the running stitch derive its name?
10. Describe the back stitch.
11. Describe the combination stitch.

CHAPTER IV

Tailors' Tacks

TAILORS' tacks are valuable to tailors and dressmakers in marking both sides of a garment so they may be exactly alike. In

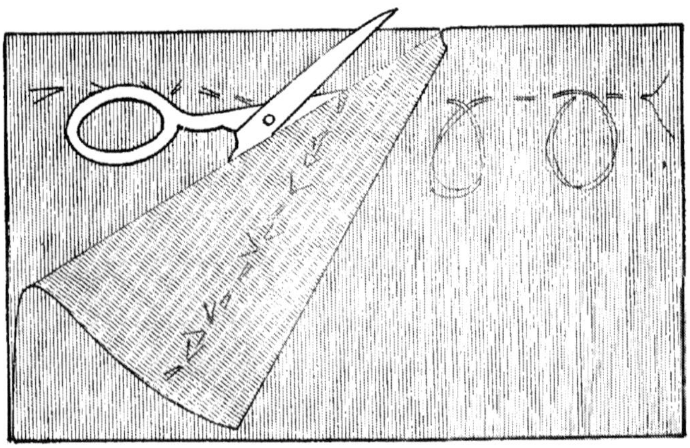

TAILORS' TACKS

putting in tucks or plaits, first-class work cannot be done without them. The stitches should be taken through both thicknesses of cloth marking them alike on both sides.

To make the stitch we use a double thread of basting cotton. Take two short stitches then leave a space a little longer than is required for the two short stitches. In this space leave a loop of the double thread two inches long. Then take two more short stitches, then loop as described and so continue until all marking for plaits, ruffles, bands, pockets, seams, or whatever it is necessary to have marking done is finished. Gently separate the edges of the material by pulling apart the mark-stitching or tailors' tacks, clip thread, being careful not to clip the goods, and separate the sides.

Over-Handing

Use over-handing to sew two edges together, usually the selvage is used.

Take stitches small and close together, over and over the seam, point needle to the left.

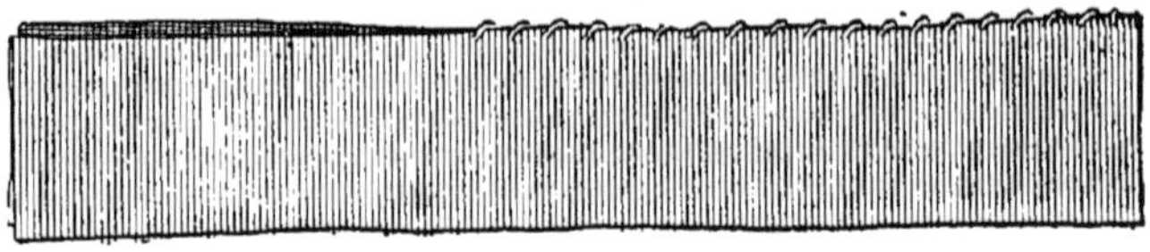

OVERHANDING

Do not draw thread too tight as it will cause the seam to pucker.

When seam is opened it should lie flat and smooth with no ridge on wrong side.

Tailors' Fell Stitch—To Sew in Lining

The fell stitch is used to sew in linings in coats and wherever an edge should be held close and stitches are not to show. This is made by bringing the threads up through the lining at the very edge. Then place needle in outside material as close to where needle comes out of lining as it can be placed. Take short stitch about one-eighth of an inch in material but not through to right side.

Again bring needle out through the edge of lining, reset as before. Do not draw thread too tight as it will cause little dents where the lining is caught.

Over-Casting

This stitch is used to keep raw edges from raveling. Trim seam even and the width it is to be finished, take a slant stitch pointing

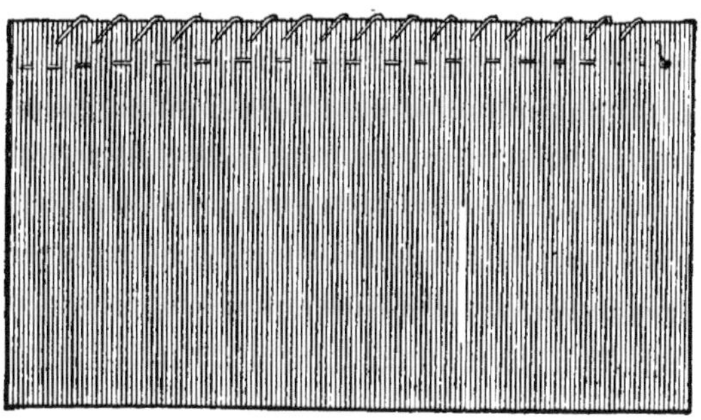

OVERCASTING

needle toward left shoulder. Loose-woven, soft material will require a deeper stitch than firm, close-woven material. An average stitch may be about one-eighth of an inch deep and one-third of an inch apart. Keep depth of stitches and space even.

French Seam

Make a narrow seam on the right side of material as narrow as material will allow.

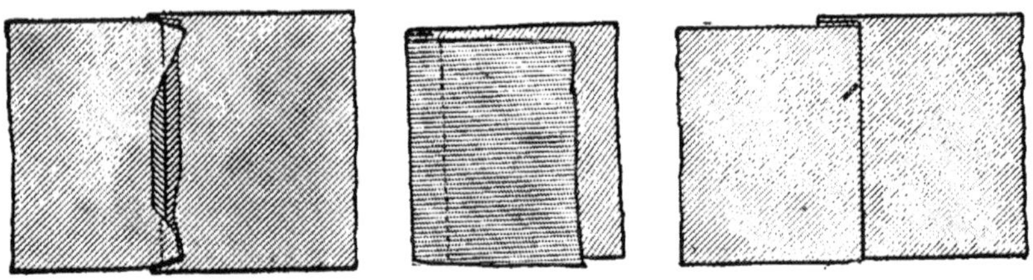

FRENCH SEAM

In fine-woven, firm material the seam may be narrower than in large thread, loose-woven goods.

Trim off all loose threads or rough edges, turn seam, crease in seam where stitching is done, baste deep enough to cover entirely the first seam and stitch again. This finish may be used on light-weight material.

Hemming

Turn edge to be hemmed from one-eighth to one-fourth of an inch, then turn width of hem desired. It should be even in width as even width and even stitches mean success to your hem. The stitches are taken on a slant, pointing needle toward the left.

On point of needle take up two or three threads of material, catching the edge of hem at same time.

Cat-Stitch or Catch-Stitch

This is a cross-stitch used as a finish to raw edge where material is heavy and flat; smooth finish is required. Take small stitch like running stitch cross-thread by working from you, alternate stitches first to the right then to the left.

Stitches should be in straight rows, one row on edge to be covered, the other just off the edge.

Feather-Stitch

Feather or brier stitching is sometimes used in place of hemming or to hold tucks in place. It may be done in single or double stitch and is very pretty as a finishing.

To make the feather-stitch have a knot in

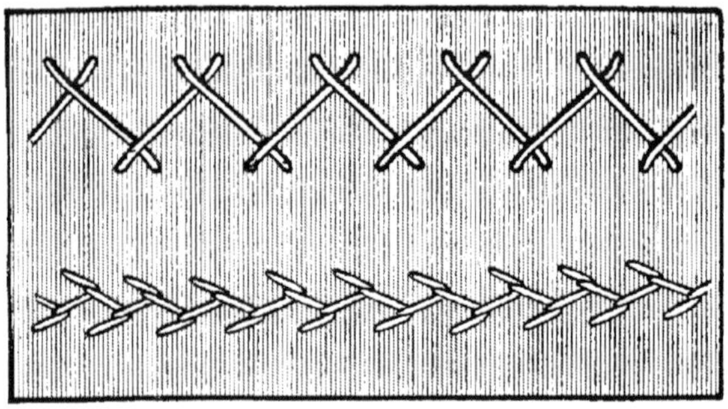

TOP—CAT-STITCH BOTTOM—FEATHER-STITCH

end of thread. Bring needle up through material, bring thread forward and place thumb of left hand on thread, take stitch placing needle about one-fourth of an inch to the right of where it was brought up through the material. Take slanting stitch about one-fourth inch long and bring needle up half-way between and one-fourth inch from where it was placed at first, bring stitch up over the thread (thread held down by thumb) continue slant stitch first to the right, then to the left and always work toward you. Two or more stitches may be taken the same slant and is very effective.

Fagoting

Fagoting is one of the prettiest stitches used in dressmaking. It is used to join edges of lace, insertion, narrow ribbon, silk or satin folds. Two folds of satin or silk may be joined with fagoting and the top fold sewed on a skirt as ornamental trimming.

The lace, fold, or ribbon should be finished and basted on paper the width apart desired, then insert the needle from the under side of each edge bringing it out over the thread, as in the feather-stitch, giving a double twist which makes it firm.

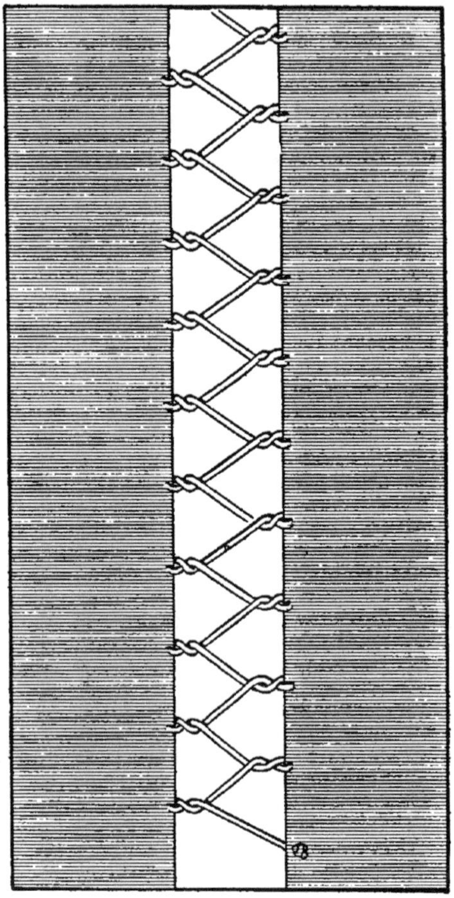

FAGOTING

Buttonhole

A nice closing is an ornament to a garment and good buttonholes help to make the successful closing.

The hem in which the buttonhole is to be made should be not less than one inch wider than the buttonhole to be worked. The straighter the edge of the buttonhole is cut, the more successful it can be made. Begin at the upper right-hand side of buttonhole. Stitches should be even distance apart and uniform depth. The depth depends on the firmness of the material; just deep enough to hold firm and not tear out.

Stitches should be close enough to keep purled edge firm and tight which makes it strong and durable.

Mark top and bottom buttonhole. Divide the space between according to the number of buttons to be used. Use buttonhole shears and cut straight, even edge for buttonhole. Bring needle up through starting point which is the upper right-hand corner, take the double thread extending from the eye of the needle and wind around needle, pull needle through and draw the thread down snug.

The front end of buttonhole should be worked round like an eyelet; the back end should be finished with bar by taking three or more stitches over each other at the end of buttonhole.

Tailored Buttonhole

In tailors' buttonhole the stitch is made the same as in the plain buttonhole in previous lesson.

The difference is in the preparation of buttonhole for working.

Determine the number of buttons to be used, find the distance they are to be apart and with the tailors' chalk mark a straight line where each buttonhole is to be worked, place a button on this line and mark with the chalk each side of the button to find the correct length of buttonhole. The buttonhole should be one-sixteenth of an inch longer than the width of button to allow the button to slip through easily.

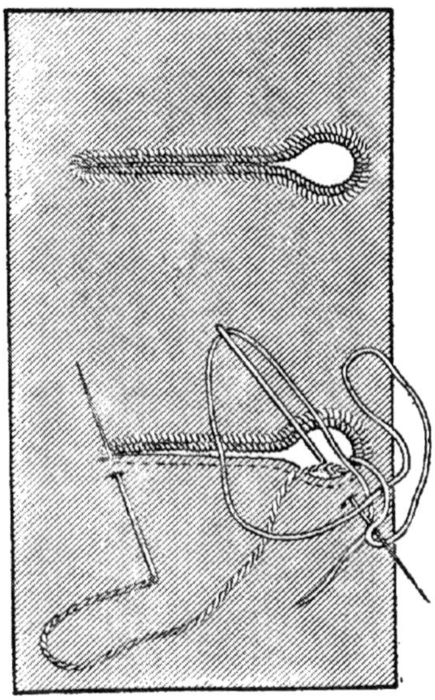

TAILORED BUTTONHOLE

Baste through all thicknesses of materials on the chalk line, use small stitches to hold material firm. Stitch each side of basting just far enough apart so that when the buttonhole is cut on basting and chalk line, in working the stitch will be taken just over the stitching.

Use buttonhole punch and punch round hole in outer edge of buttonhole, then cut with sharp shears the length marked for the opening. Use heavy linen thread in needle, then twist and double thread which gives a cord to work over. Put knot in thread, take one stitch one-eighth of an inch back of buttonhole, bring needle up at edge of buttonhole, hold this cord in place at edge of buttonhole, hold in place with left hand and work over it all around. Pull cord snug after work with silk twist is complete. Put needle through material and fasten.

Questions

1. For what are tailors' tacks used?
2. Describe the stitch used in making tailors' tacks.
3. For what is over-handing used?
4. Describe the stitch.
5. What stitch is used to sew lining in coats?
6. Describe the stitch.
7. What stitch is used to keep raw edges from raveling?
8. What kind of material requires a deep stitch.
9. Describe how to make a French seam.
10. Describe the hemming.
11. For what is the cat-stitch used?
12. Describe how to make the feather-stitch.
13. For what is it used?
14. For what is fagoting used?
15. Describe how to fagot.
16. What is the use of the buttonhole?
17. Describe how to make a buttonhole, also a tailored buttonhole.

CHAPTER V

Eyelets

EYELETS are usually used where lacing is required for the closing of a garment.

Punch a hole with a bobkin, holding work

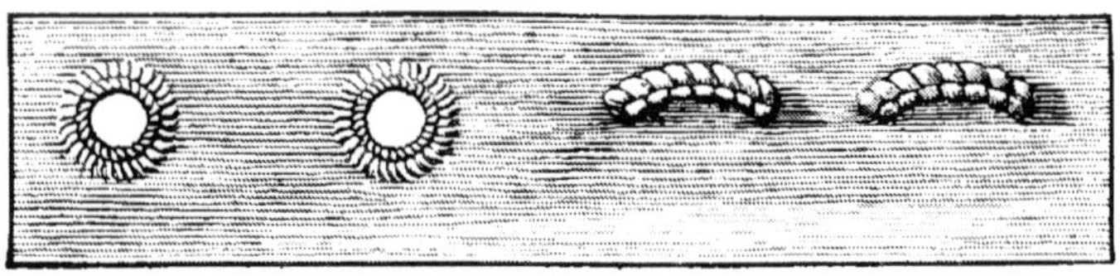

EYELETS LOOPS

in left hand, overcast, taking stitches close together to prevent the hole closing.

A very pretty eyelet is made by using the buttonhole-stitch and drawing the purl to the outer edge.

French Knots

The French knots are used as a decoration and also used on sheer material in place of beading where beads seem too heavy or on washable garments.

If the French knot is made right it washes nicely, while beads are liable to break and drop off.

Bring needle through to the right side of goods, take a tiny back-stitch, wind thread two, three, or four times around needle just above the point and with thumb of left hand hold the thread wound needle close to material. Draw needle through the material, which is still in the back-stitch just taken.

Hold thread to form knot tight against material while drawing the thread through. Take another stitch of two or three threads close to knot and the knot will wash nicely.

The number of threads wound around needle depend on the size of knot required.

Loops

Loops made of threads are sometimes necessary in closing a dress of soft material such as chiffon, lace, net, etc.

Make a bar by taking two or three stitches directly over each other and the length of the loop desired.

Use buttonhole twist or coarse thread and make buttonhole-stitch working over the bar, drawing purled edge to outer edge

Sewing on Buttons

I wonder how many of us sew buttons on correctly?

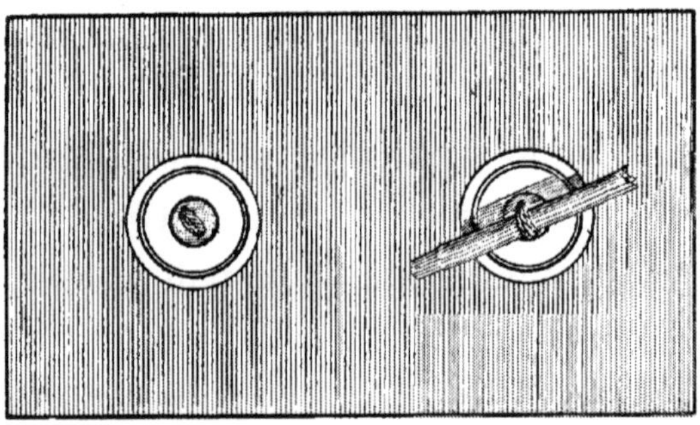

SEWING ON BUTTONS

Use as coarse thread as the material of the garment being made will allow, but always coarser than is used to make the garment.

Take two or three stitches to fasten end of thread, place button and bringing needle through one hole of button, lay across button a pin, if the button is small; if a large button, use a match or something as large, allowing thread to pass over the pin or match. After button is sewed on remove pin or match and pull button away from garment as far as possible and wind thread around under button to form a shank, which allows the buttonhole to close nicely under the button, otherwise the buttonhole spreads and gets out of shape.

Covering Molds

Cut the cover round and a little larger than the button, but not large enough to quite come together on the underside or it will be bunchy underneath.

Gather cover all around at the edge, place button in center, draw up gathering string and overhand together or nearly so.

The stitches and open space may be covered by a small piece of silk hemmed underneath.

Smocking

The honeycomb design is the one generally used.

The success of smocking depends on the marking, being precisely the same distance

SMOCKING

apart both lengthwise and crosswise, and as in all other stitches, the more even and perfect the stitches the more artistic is our finished work.

Nearly all fashion magazines sell patterns

with the spaces accurately marked for smocking. A regular desk ruler one foot in length is the most convenient for marking. Dots may be made one-fourth, one-half, or three-fourths of an inch apart. It depends on how fine the smocking to be used is to be.

It is always wise to make a small piece out of some of the pieces left in cutting the garment as you can easily change the size of smocking if you wish, while if you mark the garment and change the size afterwards you may ruin the material.

Allow about four times the width of material as smocking desired when complete.

First baste marked piece to be smocked, taking a tiny stitch of not more than four threads in each dot. Have a knot in thread and break the thread at the end of each row of dots, leaving a long end not fastened. When basting is finished take all long ends of thread and pull up as in gathers.

The marked smocking will form tucks.

Fashion usually decides what kind of stitch and what kind of thread to be used.

Sometimes thread is of different color from material used and French knots are often used to ornament where plaits are fastened together.

Hold material the right side toward you, bring needle up through first dot at right-hand top corner, fasten the next plait to this by two stitches from right to left directly over each other. Put needle through material to wrong side and take next stitch in the same way fastening the same plaits together two dots farther down skipping every other dot, begin again, skipping the first dot at top for second row and use the second and third plaits fastening together firmly skipping every other one as before, only opposite to those fastened in first plait. Continue until required width is obtained.

Sewing on Beads

Beads are always more or less used to decorate sheer, fancy gowns and blouses.

Materials generally used are Georgette crêpe, net, voile, chiffon, marquisette, and light-weight crêpe de chine when sufficiently sheer to be able to trace the lines of the design through is also used.

The pattern should be placed under the material. Smooth out both pattern and material, baste together to hold firm while sewing beads on. The thread should be the color of material. Purse silk is sometimes used as it is a little heavier than sewing silk. Sew beads on about the width of a bead apart.

There are three methods: Beads may be

strung first (placing them in a dish, thrust the needle through them; you are sure to pick up several beads at a time) and following the outline of the design use the couching-stitch and take a stitch between each bead; the running-stitch is also used, taking a few threads of material between each bead.

The most secure method is to take a back-stitch and bring the needle point out the distance of space between the beads, slip needle through the next bead and take a tiny back-stitch again to secure the bead and as before bring the needle up through the material the space between beads and continue until all are sewed on. Do not draw thread tight as it will cause all your work to pucker.

For small pieces such as ends of ribbons and scarfs, hat bands, etc., embroidery hoops are quite necessary.

French knots when made in a small knot using the colored silks to represent the beads on material where beads seem to be heavy, can scarcely be told from the beads and launder nicely.

Tailors' Pockets

One of the comforts and conveniences in a tailored dress or coat is the pocket, and just at present we are allowed pockets of all kinds and sizes.

We will give in this lesson two styles of pockets which are always used.

The pockets with a lap, which is used in coats. The lap is made first, lined, stitched, and pressed, leaving the edge unfinished that stitches to the coat. Have place marked on coat where pocket opening is to be, which is about four inches from the waistline and a little in front of the underarm seam usually two or three inches. This depends on the size of coat and most convenient place for the pocket. Baste unfinished edges of lap to upper side of mark for pocket with right side of lap toward coat, cut two pieces of coat lining one inch larger all around than pocket is to be. Baste one to lower side of mark for pocket, stitch pocket piece using one-eighth of an inch seam just the length of mark for pocket, cut slit for pockets. Turn lower piece of pocket through to wrong side, turn pocket lap down and seam on wrong side up, baste, using small stitches to hold snug, press and stitch on coat close to edge of seam above pocket lap.

Turn pocket piece (already stitched and turned through slit to wrong side) over edge of seam at lower side of pocket opening, allowing it to extend over edge of seam enough to fill space left by turning seam in lap up, baste and stitch through from right side of coat, leaving long ends of thread. After stitching pull threads through to wrong side and tie. Place the other pocket piece on the seam already turned up on wrong side, fell firmly to seam, baste pocket together, stitch, and press.

Another pocket is used in coats and skirts and one-piece tailored dresses. It can be made in different ways—straight up and down, straight crosswise, slanting or a graceful curve, not quite as strong a curve

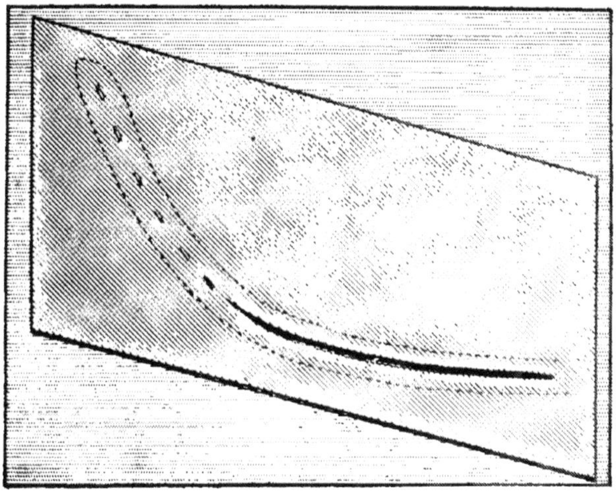

TAILORED POCKET NO. I

as a half-moon and higher at the front of pocket than the back.

Draw line with chalk whatever style the pocket is to be. Cut a piece of bias about four and one-half inches wide. If pocket is curved cut bias piece five and one-half inches wide and long enough to extend one inch over at each end of mark for pocket.

Mark pocket line strong with tailors' chalk,

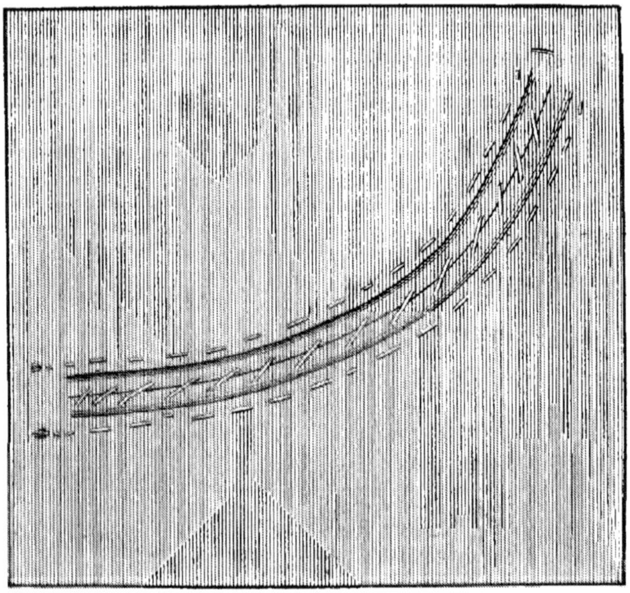

TAILORED POCKET NO. 2

lay bias piece over it and slap with the hand, this will cause the chalk mark to come off on the bias piece enough so you can see the curve. Place again on line for pocket on coat, and baste the length the pocket is to be; draw a chalk line crosswise at both ends of pocket and stitch the bias using one-eighth of an inch seam on each side. Stitch just to chalk line, being careful to have each stitching come out exactly opposite.

Leave long thread to draw through and tie to make ends of stitching firm. It is still better to back-stitch at the ends of pocket, take three or four machine stitches then raise presser foot, replace work, start again just where you started first without breaking thread, stitch to other end of pocket, back up again three or four stitches, and stitch again to the end the second time which leaves the corners of pockets strong, pull bastings, cut the line for pocket through the coat, turn facing through to wrong side and seam back from the opening on both sides of pocket.

Allow facing to form a cord on each side of pocket just enough of the loose facing to fill the space left by the seam; but no more than the eighth of an inch on each side as that was the width of seam. Baste in position turning corners neatly, overhand edges in center

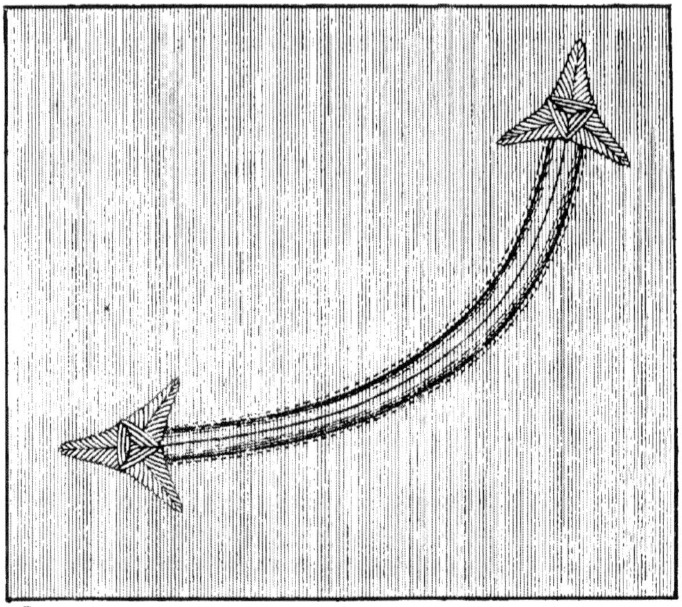

TAILORED POCKET NO. 3

together and press, cut pocket out of lining the length and width desired and sew to facing on long side, allow top of pocket to lie back toward top of coat and while in this position stitch through from the right side of the coat at edge of cord formed by facing. Leave long ends of thread at each end of pocket, pull through and tie or thread in needle and fasten securely.

Turn down top piece of pocket on the lower piece, baste, and stitch all around the edges, press pocket again and work arrow-head or crow-foot at each end of pocket.

All outside pockets should be put in coat before the lining goes in.

Bound Buttonhole

The edges of a bound buttonhole are finished the same as the pocket above, the only difference is the facing is not more than two inches wide, and are turned under on wrong side. Fell down neatly.

Patch Pocket

Dame Fashion uses patch pockets of all sizes and kinds for ornamental purposes, as well as useful ones.

These pockets should be very carefully

made, edges cut and turned even and smooth, stitching straight or the pocket will prove anything but ornamental.

The top is hemmed, bound, or lined. Sometimes in using two harmonious colors for a gown, the pocket may be lined or bound with the trimming material.

Questions

1. Where are eyelets used?
2. Describe how to make an eyelet.
3. For what are French knots used?
4. Describe how to make a French knot.
5. For what are loops used?
6. Describe how to make a loop.
7. Describe how to sew on buttons.
8. Describe how to cover button molds.
9. Explain the marking and stitching in smocking.
10. Describe how to make a tailors' pocket with a lap and one without a lap.
11. Describe the three ways of sewing on beads.
12. How should you make a bound buttonhole?
13. Describe how to make a patch pocket.

CHAPTER VI

Crow-Foot

THE crow-foot is ornamental as well as useful in plain tailored gowns. It is used to make a corner of a pocket strong and at the end of an inverted plait where it terminates at the waistline in a coat or part way down the skirt; it is also used as an ornamental finish in various ways according to the prevailing styles.

Make a triangle the desired size on the garment with tailors' chalk, drawing the line from point to point with a slight curve toward the center. Use rope silk or twist.

Bring needle up through material at outer point then take stitch at next point, taking only two or three threads of material at first stitch. Take stitch toward you, turn work in left hand outward from left to right which will seem at first backwards, but which causes the ends to cross and forms the crow-foot.

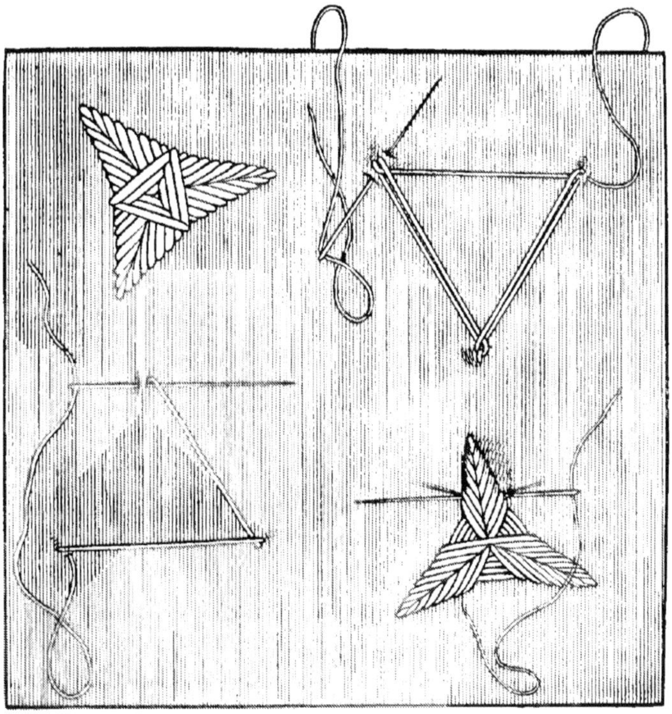

CROW-FOOT

Continue these same stitches taking them very close together and each one a thread or two longer until the center is reached, and you will find you have formed a pretty crow-foot with a surprisingly pretty center.

Arrow-Head

The arrow-head is used for the same purpose as the crow-foot. It is just a matter of choice as to which one is preferred. The diagram is made the same.

Bring needle up through at base of arrow-head to the left of where it is to cover the end of pocket or plait or seam, take stitch as for crow-foot at outer point of arrow-head, put needle down through at right point and under material, bringing it out again at left point just inside the first stitch. Again take stitch at outer point outside and just under the top stitch and two or three threads wider across as for crow-foot. Again put needle down through material just inside last stitch as before. The stitch at outer point is taken from right to left, then down through at right point which crosses the thread.

Plackets

The finish of a placket depends on the

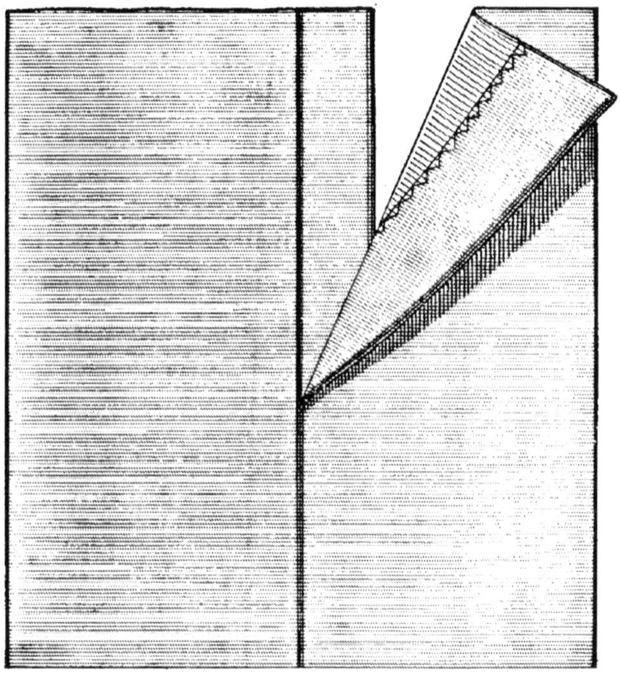

TAILORED PLACKET

fabric from which it is made also the style of the garment.

A well-made placket is of the utmost importance. The continuous placket is used for material such as thin silks, net, lace, chiffon, etc.

Make placket thirteen inches long, cut facing one and one-half inches wide and twenty-six inches long on lengthwise of material.

Pin and baste the entire length of both sides of placket, seam on wrong side. Stitch narrow seam all around placket. Pull bastings, clip seam clear to stitching at lower end of placket where facing turns. The outer edge should be turned in a seam width and folded over to just cover the machine stitching of seam just made and fell down, being careful to have stitches invisible on right side.

Placket facing should extend about one-half of an inch. Turn through to wrong side turning right side back at top, allowing left side to extend out for fly or underlap. Close with snap fasteners about one inch apart, marking where fasteners are to be placed on both sides of facing before beginning to sew them on.

This should be very carefully done as any variation in these marks may spoil the looks of the closing. Always press placket before sewing on fasteners.

In heavy material make the tailored placket. Cut one strip of material one and one-half inches wide and thirteen and one-half inches long, sew to left side of placket, seam to wrong side, face with silk, sewing facing to outer edge of under facing or fly, turn back and fell down over seam using tailor's fell-stitch as given in previous lesson. Cut strip of silk one and one-half inches wide and face back right side, press, pin placket up carefully so it lies smoothly, turn wrong side out and sew the right side facing to fly at bottom of placket, but not to the skirt.

Mark for hooks and eyes or snaps with tailors' chalk on one side of placket one inch apart. Make marks heavy, close placket, lay flat on work table, slap with hand several times. This will cause the chalk marks to mark the other side, leaving marks for hooks and eyes or snaps directly opposite each other.

In thirteen inch placket you can place the first snap or hook and eye close to the bottom, close tight with pinchers or place blotter on top after fastening this one or hooking it, hit with hammer lightly, letting it lie on flat iron. This will close it so it will not unfasten and your placket will still be long enough and never tear out at the bottom.

Where hooks and eyes are used they should be covered where they are sewed on with narrow silk or bias cut from silk. If material is heavy silk or light-weight wool facing may all be made of the goods, cutting fly double width, three inches, and right side facing one and one-half inches.

Cutting Bias

The cutting of bias is so important we cannot be too careful, whether for ruffles, milliner's folds, or the uses previously mentioned.

If bias is unevenly cut our work must be imperfect when finished. This is why "The finish begins with the beginning."

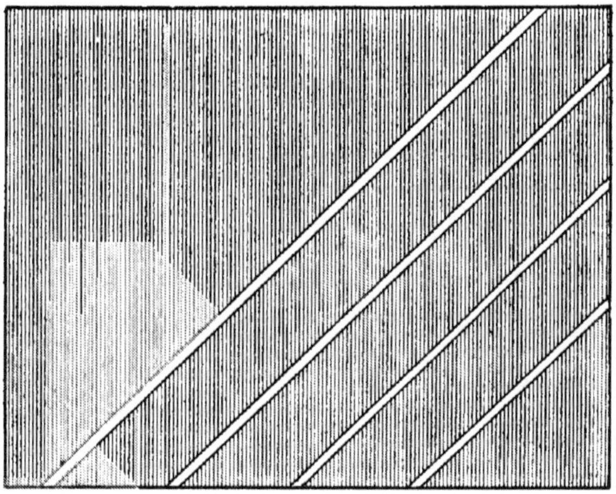

CUTTING BIAS

The selection of suitable design and material with nap running correctly, together with correct cutting in every particular and nicely worked stitches all unite in making the successful, smart garment.

In cutting the bias unfold material, place smoothly on cutting table, use a yard stick or better still a tailors' skirt rule which is forty-eight inches long and is made of good, hard wood with straight edge. The yard sticks given away for advertising are seldom straight enough to cut by.

With skirt rule mark five inches from right-hand corner on selvage edge, also five inches from same corner on cut edge with tailors' chalk or pencil. Draw line across material connecting these marks. Mark again from this line the width of bias desired and continue until sufficient bias is cut.

Shirring Bias Bands

This is very pretty trimming that Dame Fashion frequently favors and we are never sorry to see it return.

Cut bias two and one-half inches wide or more. Turn under one-half inch on each side and shirr over cord. Gather about as full as a ruffle, which is one and one-half the space to be covered. Gathered bands are sometimes put on in different designs similar to the illustration shown here.

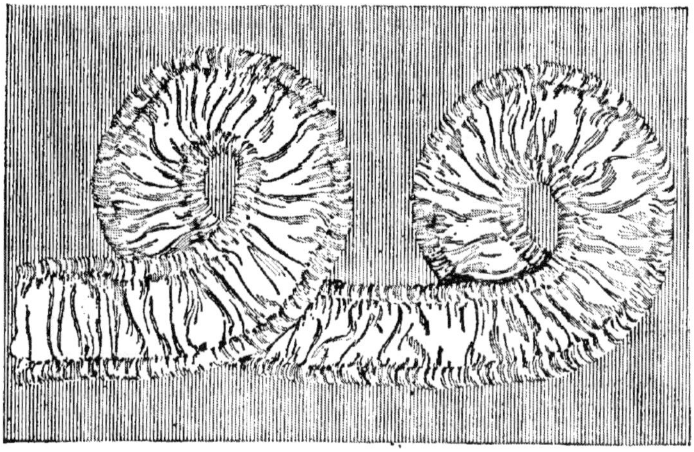

SHIRRING BIAS BANDS

Bands and Straps

Trimming bands and straps of many kinds, both crosswise and bias of various widths are used by our fashion designers at different times for ornamental purposes.

Bands are usually used on tailored skirts and coats as they retain the plain simplicity suited to the garment. They are made usually from one inch to five inches in width. The wider are used only on skirts and should be cut the shape of the skirt.

Pin gores of skirt pattern together, lay

BIAS FOLD NO. I

flat on cutting table, measure up even distance from the bottom of the skirt and mark every four or five inches all around where the band is to be applied. Connect these marks, then mark again above this line the width of band, connecting marks. Slip under skirt pattern a plain piece of paper, trace lines through on to paper, remove pattern, cut on traced lines and you have a correct pattern for a perfect fitting band.

Lay center front of pattern on fold of material when cutting.

Straps of wool material up to three inches wide finished may be cut on true bias. After edges are turned in if the skirt is circular, place band on padded pressboard, dampen lightly with wet sponge on wrong side, then with hot iron stretch one edge a little by laying bias band in circular position on board and press dry. It will retain the shape.

Bias facing when used for bottom of skirt or at back of neck in waists may be shaped the same way.

In medium weight goods, bands are usually lined with cambric or crinoline to give firmness.

Material such as taffeta, satin, etc., may be cut double the width, folding both edges at the top or if one wishes to economize they may be lined as well.

When bands are stitched on both edges, stitch the same direction on both sides of fold, for no matter how firm they are basted if stitched to the right on upper edge, then in opposite direction on lower edge, the machine crowds the band enough to make numerous little wrinkles that may press out but they come back.

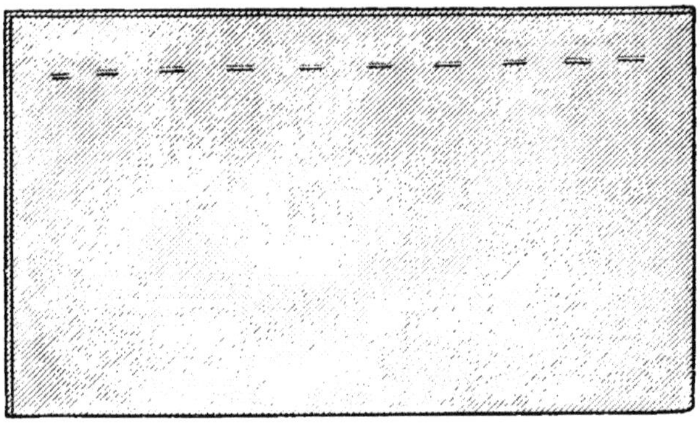

THE MATERIAL IN THE ORIGINAL MODEL FOR THIS FOLD WAS BIAS, SAME AS IN FOLD I

The beauty in all strap and fold trimming depends on even width of fold or strap, straight edges, and straight stitching.

Milliners' Folds

Milliners' folds are very ornamental when nicely made.

The width is determined by the use made of the fold. A pretty medium width is made by turning the top edge one-half to three-fourths of an inch, then turn lower edge to one-eighth of an inch of the top.

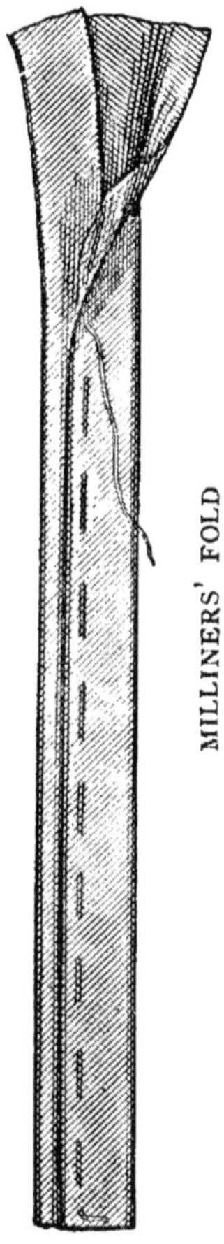
MILLINERS' FOLD

This must be straight and even, and perfectly smooth when finished.

Other wide folds for skirts, etc., can be made the same way by cutting bias the desired width and the lower edge may be turned even with the top.

For wide folds, three or four inches, when made of silk for skirt trimming, fold through center, turn both raw edges together and stitch one-eighth inch from top edge.

Questions

1. For what may the crow-foot be used?
2. What is its shape?
3. Describe how to make an arrow-head.
4. Upon what does the finish of a placket depend?
5. How long should a placket be?
6. Suggest some fitting places to use bias.
7. Explain how to cut bias strips.
8. Describe shirring bias bands.
9. For what are bands and straps used?
10. Explain how to press a bias band to fit skirt or neck.
11. Describe how to make milliners' folds.

CHAPTER VII

Couching

THIS is an over-stitch used to hold coronation braid, rattail braid, or any silk or cord used to follow an outline in embroidery.

The stitches should not be farther apart than one-fourth inch, close enough to hold the threads or cords from springing out between them.

Several threads of contrasting colors may be used with pleasing effect but should be twisted slightly in laying it on the outline. When joining or starting the braid or silk, punch a hole through the material and fasten in place.

To press when finished turn right side down on well-padded pressboard and press slowly with moderately hot iron.

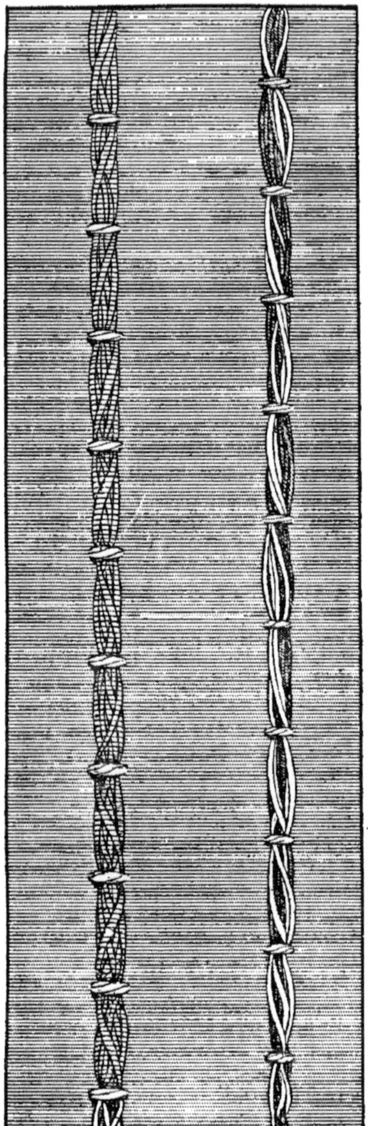

COUCHING

Covering Cord

In covering cord for ornamental purposes use a good sizable cord, say one-half to three-fourths of an inch as the cord does not appear as large when covered as before.

Soft wool may also be used if lightness of weight is desired. Cut material on true bias one inch to one and a half inches wide, this depends on the size of cord to be covered. Place cord in center of bias strip on right side of material tight around cord and take a needle's length of fine running-stitches. This determines the width of material required to cover the cord.

Draw cord out of material, then baste the length of strip keeping the same width of material as was used to cover the cord at the beginning. Use small basting-stitch, stitch on machine to make firm, being careful not to get the casing too large or too small (it is always best to make a small piece first before beginning the trimming piece), pull basting, trim

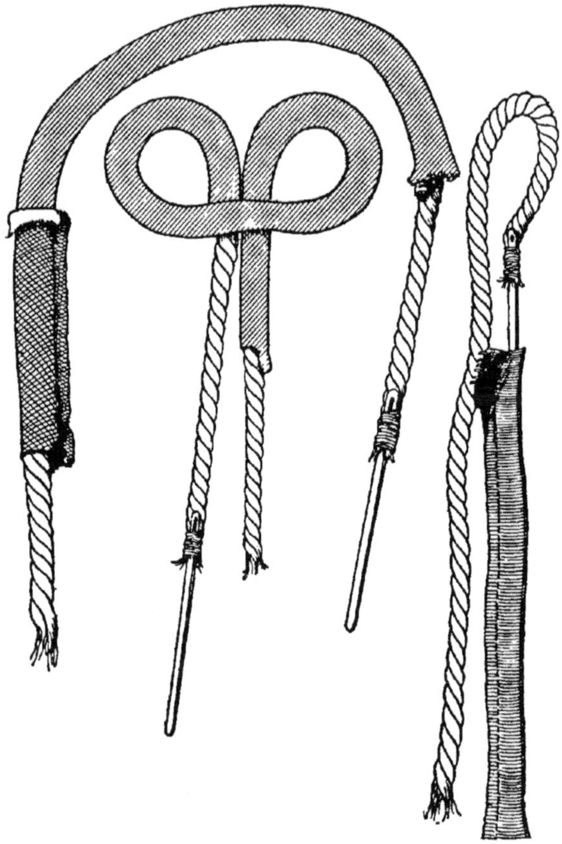

COVERING CORD

seam to an even width, being careful not to cut so close that where cord is put in it will tear out. Use tape needle and wind and sew with strong thread to the end of the tape needle as the cord is too large to go in the eye of the needle.

Sew the edge of seam in casing just made to the cord, allowing at least six inches between needle and end of casing where the sewing is done. Take stitches clear in the edge of the machine stitching from raw edge side of seam and sew very firm.

Turn tape needle back and insert in the end of casing, the casing will turn right side out over the cord as you continue to run needle in through casing.

Shirring over Cord

Material should be marked where cord is to be placed either by tracing, tailors' chalk, or mark-stitch (never use tracing wheel on silk), place cord on wrong side of material directly under marking.

With left hand hold material tight around

cord and sew by hand using a fine running-

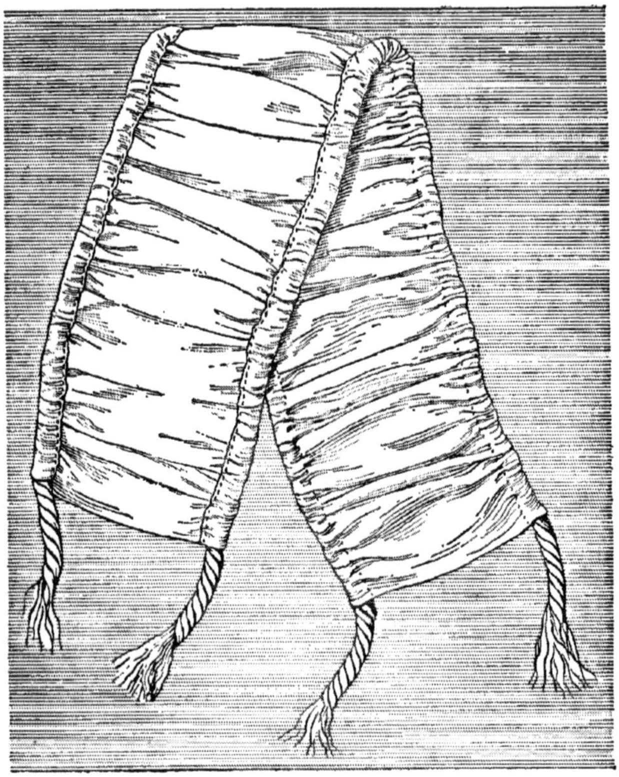

SHIRRING OVER CORD

stitch. Hold cord firmly in left hand and with right hand push material back on cord until desired fullness is obtained. Do not draw up running-stitch.

In shirring yokes or waists or skirts a number of rows of cord may be used.

Marking for Hooks and Eyes

When sewing on hooks and eyes, or snap fasteners, place them about one inch apart. Place right and left sides of garment together right side outside. They should be even top and bottom, also at waistline.

Lay flat on work table, turn back the edge of upper piece, and mark both pieces at the same time with tailors' chalk. If accurately done they will be precisely opposite and when fasteners are on, the closing will be smooth and even.

Round eyes should extend out about one-eighth of an inch. Hooks should set back from the edge one-eighth of an inch, for a placket or closing that is just to meet.

Circular Yokes

Circular yokes are occasionally very fashionable.

A yoke should be cut and fitted; and if stock collar is to be worn it also should be cut and fitted in some cheap material, such as lining cambric.

From the fitted yoke cut a paper yoke and stock and baste together.

These yokes and collars are made of lace, bias folds, two kinds of narrow lace, etc. Bias folds or lace may be basted on the paper one-half inch apart and fagoted together, or the yoke may be made of net and lace medallions appliqued on.

Net, hand embroidered, is also pretty.

To make the narrow lace yoke of two kinds of lace, valenciennes and cluny, in alternate rows, begin at the bottom of collar where it joins the yoke, baste from there to top, then outer edge of yoke allowing the edges to overlap just enough to hold.

Stitch through paper, press, and tear paper away.

Tucking Circular Skirt

Tucks in skirts are sometimes a difficult task, especially in circular skirts where the lower part of the material used in tuck is fuller than the upper.

Before the bottom can be finished the placket should be made, all seams finished, and the skirt should be finished with band or belting at the top.

Tucks require twice their length.

Find out the inches necessary for the required number of tucks to be used, pin very carefully or mark and baste the material all in one place at least half-way up the skirt the full amount to be used in tucks to get it out of the way.

Put skirt on, turn up even around the bottom, length of finished skirt.

Baste all around bottom where the skirt

turns for hem, then find the shortest place in material left at bottom for the hem.

If tucks are to graduate, being larger at

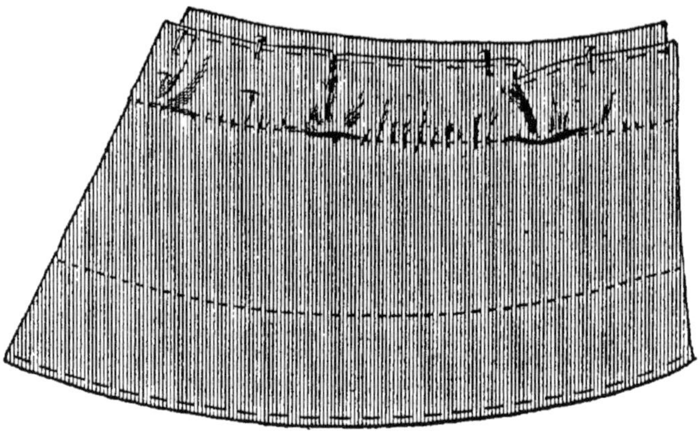

TUCKING CIRCULAR SKIRTS

the bottom and decrease in size towards the top, the hem should be as much wider than the first tuck as there is difference in the tucks; that is, if the first tuck is four and one-half inches, the next tuck three and one-half inches, then the hem should be five and one-half inches.

Mark the hem all around from where the

skirt is turned and basted at the bottom. With tape measure or a piece of cardboard with notch cut in five and one-half inches as a mark. Use tailors' chalk to mark with. It can be bought in different colors and brushes off, leaving no trace. Cut off material above mark, leaving only one-fourth inch to turn under for finish.

Turn under on chalk line and gather, using silk thread the shade of the material or any thread the dress is to be made with so this thread will not have to be removed. Use fine running-stitch, stitches to be very small, and right on edge of hem as you are to stitch through your gathering thread.

Draw up this thread to adjust the fullness and pin the hem at top until it is in proper place and gathers are where they should be for hem to lie flat and smooth, baste, and press.

Let out the goods for tucks and measure, first the distance the tucks are to be apart, then the width of tuck as the double material in tuck covers its width in material underneath it so add to the space between the tucks the width of tuck.

If tuck is four and one-half inches wide and space between tucks to be two inches, mark first notch six and one-half inches, which will be the lower part of the first tuck. Make another notch four and one-half inches above the six and one-half inch notch; this line will be the lower edge of tuck after tuck is finished.

One more notch four and one-half inches still above the notch for the center, or what is to be lower edge of finished tuck, will be the top of the tuck. Use running-stitch and as in the hem, thread the color of material so it need not be removed. Use running-stitch and stitches very small.

Run this thread all around the line six and one-half inches above the hem, turn on next line and baste the same as where hem is turned in bottom of skirt.

Lay skirt on work-table, folding on basting

that is to be lower edge of tuck, allowing top part of skirt to fall toward hem inside the skirt. The full or larger part on top, now draw up gathering thread so as to allow tuck to lay flat and smooth, pin all around to position, turn tuck down to inspect work and see if it looks right; if not, re-adjust gathers and pin them, then baste. Proceed in like manner for balance of tucks and you will find the result most charming and satisfactory.

Questions

1. For what is the couching-stitch used?
2. Describe "Covering Cord."
3. Describe "Shirring over Cord."
4. How far apart should hooks and eyes or fasteners be placed?
5. Explain how to mark for hooks and eyes or fasteners.
6. Explain how to make a circular yoke.
7. Give directions for tucking a circular skirt.
8. Explain how to finish the top of a skirt.

CHAPTER VIII

Getting the Length of the Skirt

AFTER a skirt has been properly finished at the top, hooks and eyes on and can be put on firmly as it will be worn, there are two good ways to get the length.

One is to use a yard stick, placing one end on the floor as far from the feet as the skirt hangs away from the figure, but keep it the same distance in front and front side, then as you near the side back, set your yard stick a little farther from the feet, and still a little farther across the back.

This will be guaged by the fullness in the skirt, a circular skirt has more fullness to the side back and back, causing it to stand farther away from the figure where the greater amount of fullness is and also to be shorter the farther its stands away.

If the yard stick is kept the same distance from the feet all around, the back of the skirt will appear shorter than the front. Allow the yard stick to rest against the figure at the top and place a pin at that point. Move the yard stick two or three inches and pin again at top, continue until you have pinned all around the skirt.

Try to stand in a natural and erect position while this is being done as every movement of the figure changes the adjustment at the bottom.

Remove the skirt, place it on work-table, and place yard stick with small numbers at the top and the same number of inches above the line of pins that were just put in at the top of the skirt, as you wish your skirt to be shortened at the bottom, then mark with tailors' chalk at the bottom of the yard stick every three inches all around the skirt, turn skirt up on this line and pin at edge where it is turned, again at edge of material turned up.

Try skirt on to see if it is just even around the bottom.

Always try to keep one position while the skirt is being turned up as it will not hang even unless you do.

Another way to turn up a skirt even is to use a skirt guage and chalk or turn and pin all around while the skirt is on, moving skirt guage around skirt and pinning about three inches apart. After the skirt is pinned up even baste on lower edge, find the narrowest place in material for hem, then measure at this point, allowing enough to turn raw edge well under. With tape line measure from bottom of skirt, this distance all around the skirt, cut off all extra material above mark except enough to turn raw edge under.

Turn on chalk line, use running-stitch, take small stitches, and run gathering thread all around at edge where the skirt is turned on chalk line. Draw thread up where it is necessary to make it fit the skirt, pin to place and baste.

Press with damp press cloth and stitch.

After stitching press again on right side (see subject of pressing).

Basting in a Sleeve

Run gathering thread all around top of sleeve, hold sleeve toward you, place sleeve

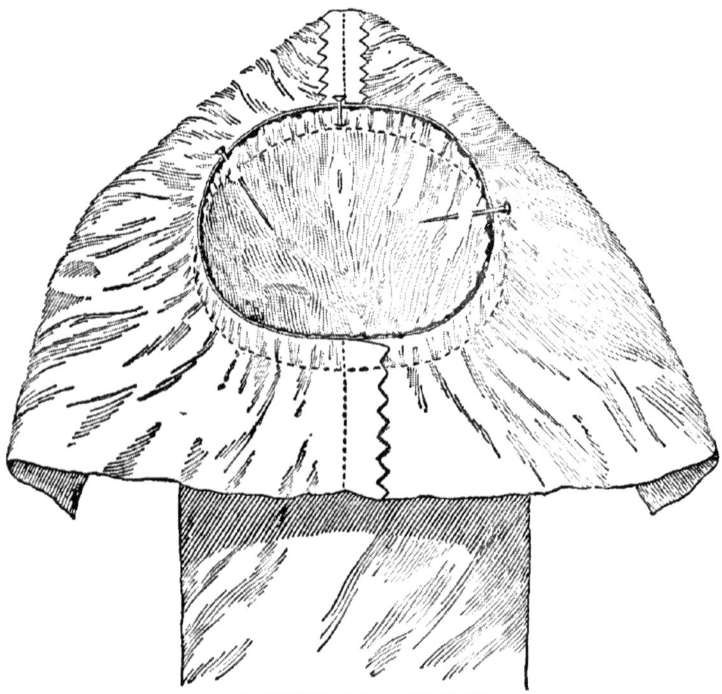

BASTING IN A SLEEVE

so that center of lowest point of sleeve is pinned to lowest point of armhole under arm; and center of highest point of sleeve to center of highest point of armhole.

Adjust gathers so that sleeve will be eased in all around but a little stronger at top than remainder of sleeve.

If sleeve is large it should be eased in under arm and about half-way up the armhole, then the balance gathered in across the top and half-way down the sides. It is very important that the sleeve be held toward you while the work is being done.

Try sleeve on before stitching as it is sometimes necessary to make a change as all arms and shoulders are not just alike.

In real round shoulders the top of the sleeve has to set farther forward than in straight shoulders.

When fitting the sleeve see that the elbow comes in the right place, also that the center of top of sleeve at highest point on top.

Tailor's Seams

The finish of tailored seams differ according to style adopted.

Even, straight stitching is absolutely necessary in tailoring which can be done with less practice than the student will at first suppose.

Concentration while you work, is of the utmost importance.

Bound Open Welt

Allow one-half to three-fourths of an inch seam, pin, baste, and stitch seam in regular way.

Remove basting, trim off one side of material, turn the wide side over the trimmed edge, turning outer edge under the same as a hem, keep it smooth and even.

Baste and stitch on outer edge. This finish is for unlined garments. In lined garments the edges are left raw.

Strap Seam

Strap seams are frequently used in the finish of unlined coats made of silk, linen, or wool.

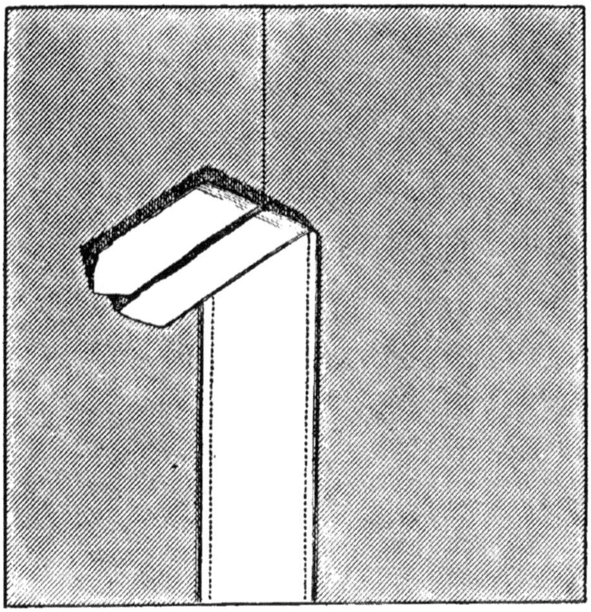

STRAP SEAM

If coat is unlined baste so raw edges of seam come on right side.

After stitching trim seams off to one-fourth

of an inch and press open. Cut strap one and one-half inches wide, either cross-wise or bias, fold edges under, leaving finished strap three-fourths of an inch wide, baste, and press. Place center of strap over center of seam, pin, baste, and stitch.

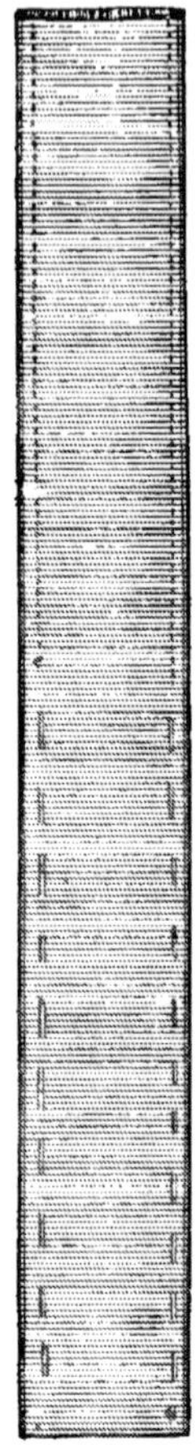

STRAP FOR SEAM

Lined coats are also finished with straps, only when lined, the raw edges of the seams are on the wrong side of the garment, and the straps made, pressed, and center of strap over seam on right side of garment.

Suit skirts in tailor work should have the same finish and trimming as the coat.

Imitation Strap Seam

This finish is especially good for unlined garments.

Mark-stitch seam as usual, lap seam placing mark-stitching directly over each other, pin and baste on mark-stitching, turn edges

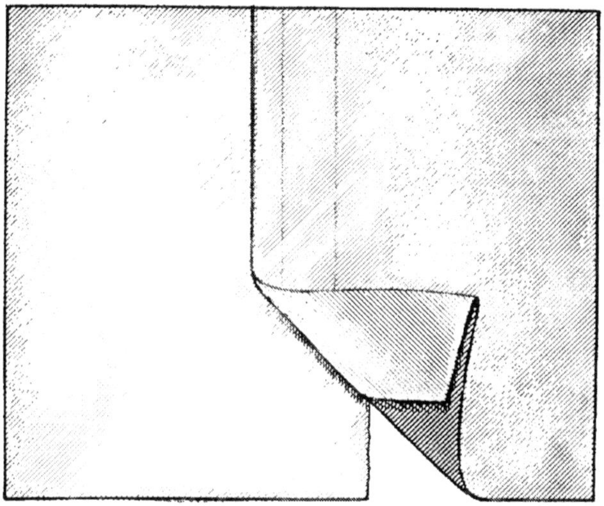

IMITATION STRAP SEAM

of seam under and baste on both wrong and right side of garment. Stitch seam at edge where it is turned under. Be particular to have turning even.

Press before stitching.

Questions

1. What must be done to a skirt before getting the length?
2. Describe how to get the length of a skirt with a yard stick.
3. Describe how to get the length of a skirt with a skirt gauge.
4. Describe how to pin and baste in a sleeve.
5. How does the finish of tailored seams differ?
6. How can one become proficient in stitching?
7. Is the stitching of tailored seams important?
8. Describe a welt seam.
9. Describe a strap seam.
10. Describe an imitation strap seam.

CHAPTER IX

Slot Seam

ALLOW one and a half inch seam. Pin and baste, press seam open.

Cut a piece of material on the crosswise of

SLOT SEAM

goods three inches wide, lay flat underneath with center of three-inch piece over center of same.

Pin and baste one-fourth to one-half inch from the edge, turn garment to right side, mark one inch or the desired width of slot seam from center and stitch.

Press and pull bastings?

Occasionally slot seams have two stitchings each side of the slot.

Raw Edge Lap Seam

This seam is usually used on heavy mate-

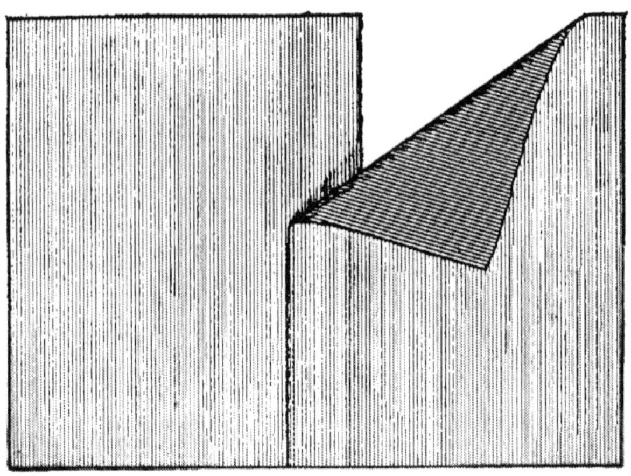

RAW EDGE LAP SEAM

rial especially those that do not ravel like melton, beaver, and other thick, firm cloth.

It is sometimes used for broadcloth.

Mark-stitch seams as usual lap seam, placing the mark-stitchings directly over each other, pin, and baste seam. Baste seam again at outer edge and again on mark-stitching on opposite side of mark-stitching, making space between stitching one-half inch or more.

As Fashion is a fickle goddess and changes almost while our gowns are being made, it is necessary to note what style of seam finish is in use and adopt it. This is why we should know all the different seam finishings and be ready for our fickle friend.

Fell Seam

This seam is a fell, hemmed down to hide a raw edge.

Trim off one edge of the seam close to the stitching, turn under the other edge, press with thumb, baste, and hem. This is used in

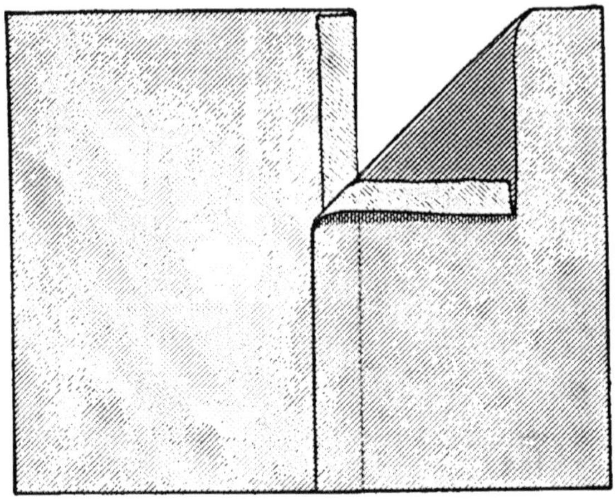

FELL SEAM

making up wash goods and other light material, including silk.

Matching Flowers and Stripes

In flowers note if there is an up and down to the flower; stems usually run down.

As in plaids, if goods is wide and can be folded see that the flowers are exactly opposite before cutting.

If narrow material cut one-half of the garment, then lay all cut pieces on material for the other half of dress, right sides together, being careful that flowers all run the same direction and come opposite the flowers in the pieces already cut.

Stripes should also be carefully cut. Be sure the center of a stripe comes in the center back, also center front of the garment, and stripes on right and left side match also where the joining comes in gored skirts.

It is well to cut front gore first, then place pattern of next gore and lay front gore by it to see if the stripes match. If not, move pattern until they do match. Continue in like manner until all gores are cut.

Matching Plaids

When plaid material is wide enough to cut double, be sure it is folded in the center of a plaid so that all plaids match as they face each other in the folded material.

If necessary to cut single, after the right

side is cut, place all cut pieces on the material right sides together, plaids matching. In this way no two pieces will ever be cut for one side.

If a one-piece dress the crosswise plaids should match at waistline in front, back, and under arm.

In cutting a waist match plaids at bust line.

In matching plaids at seams it is sometimes necessary to place piece over one-half or full width of a plaid to have the stripes match correctly.

More material is always required in plaid, figures, flowered or material with nap, than plaid material with no nap.

In plaids cut front of skirt or waist, then lay cut pieces on material against pattern as it is lain on for next gore and see if plaids match. If they do not, move pattern until they do match.

Questions

1. Describe a slot seam.
2. What materials are suitable for raw edge lap seams?
3. Describe a raw edge lap seam.
4. What good reason would you suggest for learning all seam finishings?
5. Describe a fell seam.
6. How should a skirt be pinned on the figure in the first of the fitting?
7. In case hips are not alike how may the defect be remedied?
8. Should a skirt be a trifle larger around at the waistline than belting?
9. How would you prevent a skirt from swinging front?
10. When are you ready to get the correct length of a skirt?
11. Describe how to match flowers and stripes in cutting a garment.
12. Describe how to match plaids.

CHAPTER X

Cutting a Garment so as Not to Have Two Pieces for One Side

ALWAYS cut with right side of material facing each other.

If material is narrow and it is necessary to cut single, cut all the pieces for one side, then lay them on material right sides together and cut for the other side.

This will always give you right and left side of all pieces cut, which is absolutely necessary or both sleeves would be for one arm and the whole dress for one side.

Length of Skirt for Girls at Different Ages

This is quite a problem to the mother and also to the girls themselves. The rule given here will vary in older girls from thirteen years of age, according to their growth and development.

From three to five years the dress should just cover the knee. The child of average growth may continue this length until eleven or twelve years old, then the dress should be two inches longer.

At fourteen, if she is very small for her age, she may still wear the same length but if well developed the skirt should just cover the top of the calf or largest part of the leg in the back. If unusually tall the skirt may be an inch or two longer.

At fifteen it should be two inches longer, and from sixteen to eighteen the skirt should be to the top of the shoe, unless the prevailing fashion determines the length of dresses to be as short as they are at present; if so, she may wear whatever length is the style, providing it is becoming and her mother is willing.

Acid Test for Cloth

To test silk boil the same in five per cent solution of caustic potash for fifteen minutes.

If the silk is pure the fabric will be practically destroyed leaving but a small residue like paper ashes. If there is cotton in it, the cotton will remain.

Another excellent test is to remove the threads which form the warp and the woof. Keep these separately and test them in strong hydrochloric or sulphuric acid. If they are pure silk the threads will dissolve within two minutes.

If there is either wool or cotton in the fabric the threads will remain unaffected.

Pure woolens are adulterated even more than silk because they are in greater demand, and also because they are quite easy to imitate.

Many a yard of cloth sold as "pure wool" contains from thirty to sixty per cent cotton. Blankets sold as "half wool" have frequently been found to contain only ten per cent of pure wool.

There are machines to-day which cleverly wrap wool around cotton thread and the finished product has every appearance of being "all wool."

Another method of adulteration is by taking cotton cloth and "felting" short woolen threads upon its surface by means of heat, moisture, and pressure.

A purchaser may be fully convinced from appearance and feeling of cloth that it is all wool, but the only safe method is to take home samples and make tests.

Immerse the samples of so-called wool in oil of vitriol for about two minutes. This will destroy the cotton but the wool will not be affected.

Another test is to moisten a sample with fifty per cent nitric acid. This will turn the wool yellow but the cotton will retain its color. Use the same tests for linens as you do for woolens. If the sample is genuine linen it will not be affected by oil of vitriol, but any cotton that is in it will be destroyed.

Imitation damask is made to-day by means of printing upon the surface with a sort of transparent mucilage the designs. By immersing a sample in hot boiling water and allowing it to boil several minutes the design will disappear.

Questions

1. How should you fold material in cutting so both pieces of garment will not be cut for one side?
2. In case material is too narrow to fold what would you suggest to prevent cutting two pieces for one side?
3. What length is suitable for girls from three to five years to wear their skirts?
4. Should all girls of thirteen years of age wear skirts the same length?
5. Who is best fitted to decide the length of a girl's skirt?
6. What is the usual length approved of for girls of fourteen?
7. Suggest an acid test for silk.
8. Suggest ways that wool may be adulterated.
9. How may we test wool?
10. How may we test linen?

CHAPTER XI

Pressing

PRESSING is not ironing. In pressing after sponging always press with the threads of material lengthwise, this helps to keep material smooth and straight, in good shape for cutting.

All outside seams should be pressed before stitching, such as plaits in skirts, hems, facings, cuffs, collars, etc.

It will be very noticeable how much easier it is to stitch.

After stitching press again over the stitching, otherwise there will be an unfinished look where stitching is done. This pressing over the stitching should be done on the right side, using press cloth which should be a piece of heavy unbleached muslin, at least one yard with no dressing on it. If you find, after you have bought it, it gets stiff and sticks to the iron, have it laundered to take out the dressing, then your press cloth is ready for use. Nearly all pressing is done over a damp press cloth.

In some cases, with such material as broadcloth, two thicknesses of the dry press cloth is put next the material, then the damp press cloth on top. This steams the material instead of wetting it and does not take the luster off.

Too much stress cannot be applied to the importance of good pressing. A pressing iron should weigh at least twelve pounds; the weight is quite important.

Do not take hold of a seam ahead of iron and pull on it to straighten it out or you will stretch the seam in pressing.

Open the seam but allow material to remain smooth in a natural position.

In semi-fitted dresses and coats the little crosswise wrinkles that are apt to come in the gores between the seams at waist line, can be removed by dampening the seam with a wet sponge and stretch with a pressing iron from two inches above to two inches below the waistline. Do not have the iron too hot so it will scorch (try it on a piece of material to make sure you will not burn your garment). Do not move the iron all the time as in ironing.

Be sure it will not burn, then let it rest until you think the material is pressed dry underneath. Always press material until thoroughly dry, then move iron one length ahead.

To Take Shine off Worn Garments, or from Pressing

To remove the shine caused by pressing the following suggestions will prove helpful.

When the garment is finished and thoroughly pressed there is liable to be a gloss or shine on places where heavy pressing is done. This may be removed by steaming and brushing.

Dip one end of press cloth in water, using dry as you can wring it; place one thickness of dry sponge cloth over the material, then the damp cloth, having the pressing iron very hot. Move quickly back and forth over the wet muslin two or three times, remove, have whisk broom ready, and while steaming brush briskly and you will find the mark of pressing gone.

In serge and other hard twill material that become shiny with wear, if the steaming process does not remove it satisfactory, use a fine sandpaper and ruff the material a little.

This shine is caused by all fiber ends of material, which is nap, being pressed down or worn off smooth.

Finishing Top of Skirt

After the skirt is fitted and stitched finish the seams by binding, notching, or overcasting.

Put upper and under facing on placket as taught in subject on plackets, press, and inspect your work to be sure it is correctly done.

Now we are ready to put the skirt on the band or belt. A skirt should always be eased into the band or belting, as it gives an easy natural fitting skirt. I do not mean a gathered skirt but the skirt should be a little larger than the band or belting so as to ease onto it, the belting a little tighter than the skirt.

If the belting is used it should be made just the size of the waist unless very wide, like three inches, then it should be about one inch larger and little darts, about four or five on a side, should be taken in the bottom of the belting. Take up as small a seam as can be by machine and graduate to a point about one and one-half inches from the edge. This makes the belting large enough at top and keeps it from slipping too far below the waistline at the bottom. Finish the ends of the belt with a hem. Do not have belting large enough to lap.

Put hooks and eyes on allowing round eyes to extend out one-eighth inch and hooks to set back from the edge the same distance. This will bring the belting just to meet but not lap. Close and pin placket.

The right side of the belting should have the hooks on, the left side the eyes, as all plackets close from right to left. Leave placket closed and pinned to place full length. Place belting so the left side with eyes on will come to the edge or extension of under side of placket.

Find center of front and back of skirt, also center of front and back of belting, pin centers together, allowing the skirt to extend one-half inch above the belting. Pin from center front to center back easing in a little to have the skirt fit nicely. Fit the skirt again to see if it hangs well and if it swings front at the bottom in front while on the figure remove pins at back and lift the skirt a little to correct the trouble.

The lifting of the skirt may make it a little

too large at waistline and you may be obliged to take it in at the top again.

The one-half inch of material left at the top of skirt may be turned over belting to wrong side and basted down. Stitch skirt through the belting and material from right side close to the edge. Finish raw edge by trimming off frayed edges even width all around.

If material is light weight, turn under edge and cat-stitch or fell. If heavy it should be covered with a piece of bias in cotton or silk and edges felled to belting. The bias piece should extend beyond the belting on the right side of placket where the skirt laps.

Questions

1. In pressing should we move the iron with the crosswise or lengthwise thread?

2. Should outside seams be pressed before stitching?

3. Is it necessary to press again after stitching?

4. On which side should this last pressing be done?

5. What kind of cloth would you suggest for a "press cloth?"

6. Give directions for pressing broadcloth.

7. Is pressing necessary to a perfect finish of a garment?

8. What weight should a pressing iron be?

9. How may wrinkles at waistline be successfully removed?

10. How would you suggest removing the shine in serge and other hard twill materials?

11. What causes the shine?

12. Give directions for finishing the top of a skirt.

CHAPTER XII

Lines

THE lines of a gown mean gracefulness and artistic becoming effect from the top of the collar to the bottom of the hem.

I am pleased to note that there are few, yet some of them still exist, who think if they can only keep the waist a certain number of inches and quote it often, that no matter how much fat bulges out over the top and bottom of the corset they are still slender and girlish.

This type of woman wants her dresses all fitted tight, especially across the bust and around the hips, believing she makes herself look small, when she is only emphasizing the fact that she is stout. She looks as if she had outgrown her clothes, drawing attention to what she wishes to conceal.

One can never look well in a tight corset with the flesh bulging above and below.

A first-class modiste will refuse to make a gown if her customer is not properly corseted, because she would send out a piece of work that would hurt her establishment. She could not make good lines.

No gown or suit is ever stylish or smart unless becoming.

Loose, comfortable-fitting, graceful lines conceal while tightness emphasizes.

It is as essential for the stout woman to dress loosely as the extremely small figure, the designs should be entirely different but both types would be improved.

We have all noticed the middle-aged or elderly woman with clothing too tight; her large arms, short neck, and abdomen protruding. This unsightliness is usually due to tight corseting and the tight clothing makes an exhibit of what the poor woman thinks to conceal.

No gown maker should attempt to build a gown on such a foundation.

I once read an article on dress from one of our great European designers which I have never forgotten. He said: "I'd rather people did not buy my gowns or wear my designs than to mutilate them by poor fitting, making them too tight, or wearing hats or shoes that spoil them."

If you see an exceptional, smart costume on the street, notice hat, gloves, and shoes form part of the whole costume and look as if they were a part of it; then look again and you will see that the person wearing the gown has correct lines underneath, or if not correct, they have been carefully and artistically concealed by the fitting.

A well-made, good-fitting corset is all important and should be the first consideration.

There are some things that we cannot afford and some things we cannot afford to go without.

Combining Colors

In combining colors nature never makes a mistake.

The usual, pleasing combinations that the French produce are a careful study of nature's art in combining colors.

A walk through your own flower garden, the park or woods in summer, will furnish all the color hints you could desire.

I have heard it said, a weaver in trying to reproduce a piece of beautiful moss on his loom found he had produced velvet.

Putting Canvas in Front of Coat

All linen canvas must be shrunken. You will need a yard and a half to two yards of soft linen canvas of good weight, but not stiff with dressing, the amount depends on the length of coat.

Cut the linen for facing on a four-inch bias. This is done by placing the pattern for facing on the linen with one end of front edge of pattern four inches from the edge of linen,

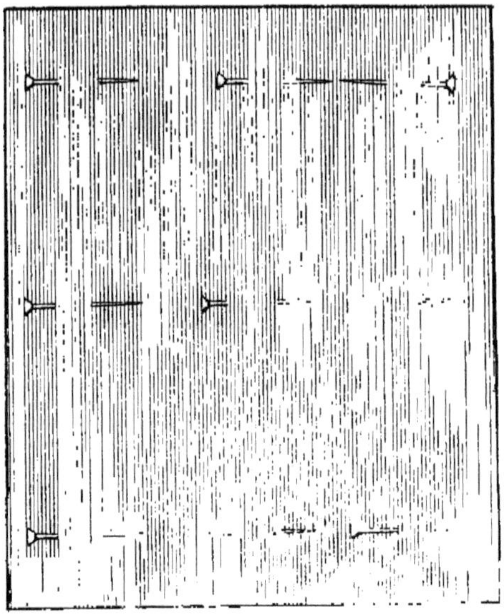

PINNING CANVAS IN FRONT OF COAT

giving a four-inch slant from top to bottom on front edge of linen.

Linen facing should be cut as wide as coat facing is to be.

Place linen on work-table, then coat front on top with front edges, neck, and shoulder even, pin across at neck and shoulder, pins about two inches apart. Place one hand on garment where pins are holding coat firmly on table, with the other hand brush coat down tight over linen, pin again about four inches below the first pinning across facing. Continue the same process to the bottom of coat. You will find when finished the linen is slack and coat material tight on linen. This is as it should be, as all interlinings as well as linings in coats must be easy or slack inside.

Leave coat front in same position with linen underneath and baste together using the diagonal or bias basting as taught in previous lesson, basting from top to bottom, first row (taking the stitches toward you), the second row from bottom to top, and continue back and forth until the linen is firmly basted on.

Remove pins, crease edge by turning a seam's width, basting and pressing the entire length of front edge across top of revere. Pull bastings and tape front of coat.

The tape should be narrow linen tape about

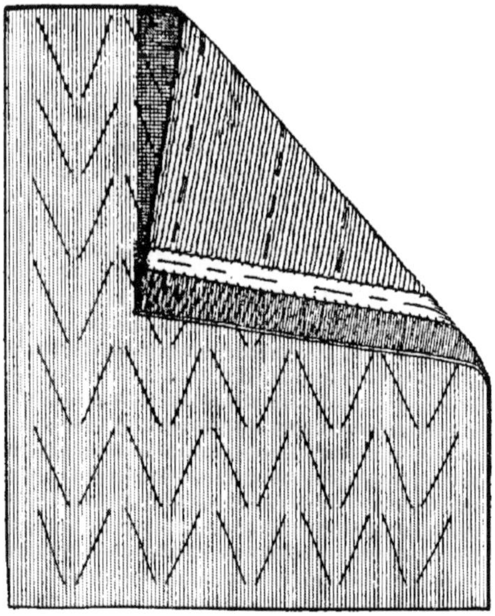

BASTING AND TAPING FRONT OF COAT

one-fourth inch wide and well shrunken before using.

Pin tape from top to bottom of coat so it will be snug on the linen about the same as the material or nearly so. Pin edge of tape on crease just made a seam's width from the edge, place tape inside the crease as the linen outside is to be cut away before stitching.

Baste tape. The part that turns over for the revere should be caught to the material by numerous rows of the padding-stitch. Just catch into the coat. Pin tape on the line of turning for revere. This tape should be a little tight to prevent stretching. Try coat on and if coat swings back at bottom pin tape a little tighter in front of coat.

If coat swings too far over it is too tight and should be loosened a little at front edge. Now sew, using overhand-stitch, over and over the edge of tape, placing needle close to tape for each stitch and not through to show on right side of material.

Pin facing on, placing the right side to right side of coat. Pin this on so it is a little easier than the coat material, baste on outer edge of tape, cut away canvas on outside of the tape, and stitch the edges of coat and facing together one-eighth of an inch beyond the edge of tape and linen.

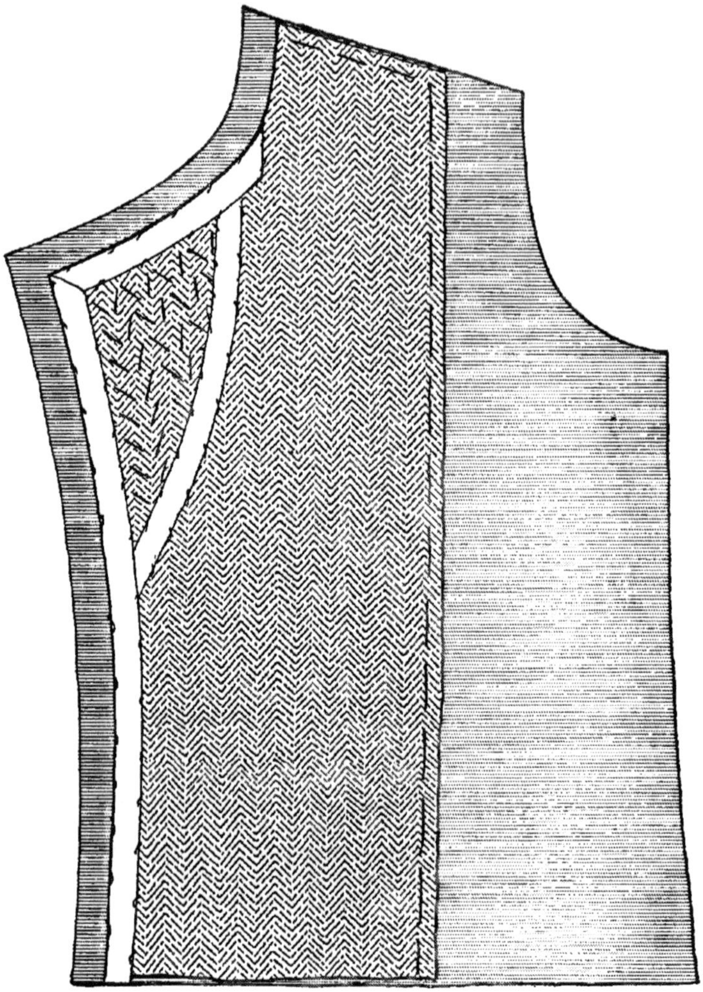

THE LINING OF THE COAT

Pull basting, cut away one-half of the seam on one edge, which should be the edge of the coat proper.

Press seam open flat.

Turn both edges of seam (but not the facing) over on tape and canvas being careful to have edge flat and smooth in the turning, and the narrow edge of seam you just turned off should lie underneath the wide side of full-width seam.

Cat-stitch firmly to linen. Turn facing, crease in line of stitching, and baste along edge of coat, also seam. Hold work in left hand and baste the entire facing over the linen, using the diagonal basting as you did to baste the linen to front of coat, only this time you hold the work over the left hand slightly rolling to have the facing basted in easy.

Miscellaneous

Stitch against the pile in velvets, plushes, and corduroy, and seams are less noticeable.

Clip basting every three or four inches and remove as soon as stitching is done.

In silks, velvets, broadcloths, and many other materials a long basting pulled out is liable to make holes or even tear the material.

To put collar on a dress or coat, find center back of garment and collar, pin together at this point then pin from the center back to the right end and from the center back to the left, and if the collar does not come cut even in front you did not locate the center back carefully. Try again.

When cutting a garment, if no seam or fold of material comes directly in front or back in waist or skirt, the centers should be marked by mark-stitching or tracing the full length of waist and skirt as it is necessary in fitting to place centers in correct position on the figure, also in joining waist, skirt, and belt to have centers meet correctly.

A careful and painstaking beginning brings successful ending.

A little extra marking, observing all notches, reading all instructions that come with the pattern, as they are important, will save so much trouble later on in the making of the garment.

About Basting

A New York tailor, at the head of a large establishment, gave the estimate of the time consumed in the proper basting of a lady's coat, by a first-class workman, to be twenty hours' work, while the machine stitching could be done in one hour, yet the average dressmaker thinks basting a waste of time. If such dressmakers will try thorough basting with a short needle, basting with short stitches, about one-fourth inch long (I have seen them from an inch to an inch and a half long) they will be able to notice much improvement in their own work.

This is why it is said a woman cannot make a tailored suit, also why they are called "dressmaker's coats."

There are many women in the tailoring business that do work equal to the best done by men, but they are never out of a position, or are doing a profitable business themselves, so we only hear about the less successful ones.

It is as important in good dressmaking to do thorough, painstaking work as in tailoring, therefore never slight your basting.

Press cushions are made about the shape of an egg, only not quite so rounding on top and about fifteen inches long, and seven and one-half inches wide. They may be stuffed with saw-dust, cork, or light-colored woolens, cut in small pieces. This pad is quite necessary in pressing curved seams; also a pad smaller, about one-third or one-half the size, that will fit in the upper part of sleeve and shoulder when pressing.

All braid should be shrunk before using.

Cleaning Black Silk

Use the kitchen table that has no finish.

Brush out and dust material. Lay flat on table, have ready for use some strong cold tea and a sponge. Lay piece of silk flat on table, brush or rub lightly with sponge, wet in cold tea. The silk will cling to the table; rub lightly on both sides, smooth out with the hand, and leave it on the table until dry. It will look like new. Do not press; it will not need pressing if left to thoroughly dry.

Soap bark is fine to use in washing all wool materials, especially in black or colors, as it will not take out the color or injure the fabric.

To remove machine oil, especially from silk, place a blotter under and over the oil spot, place a moderately hot iron on top and leave it there. The oil will be drawn out into the blotter.

Buckles are sometimes used, made of the same material as the dress to catch up a drapery or hold material in place. To make foundation, draw and cut a pattern the size and style you wish. Cut out of cardboard. First cover the cardboard with a bit of sheet wadding, then the material may be wound, plaited, or gathered on.

Foundations may also be made in buckram and if not stiff enough wired, then they will bend in shape. They are sometimes covered with beads or other trimmings.

Selvages are liable to draw. Either cut them away or clip the edges to prevent bad results.

To prevent thread knotting or snarling while sewing, after you have brcken off the thread from the spool, hold ends tight in both hands and stretch before using.

In stitching thin silk, chiffons, crêpe de chine, etc., that are liable to pucker while the stitching is being done, place a narrow strip of paper under the material and pay no special attention to it only to see that it remains over the feed and stitch as if it were not there.

Basting is to hold material firmly in place while the fitting and stitching is being done.

If carelessly basted with too long, crooked stitches, the material will not hold well in place while stitching is being done and the result is anything but satisfactory. We will have work that looks home-made instead of professional.

When tight lining is necessary, for sheer dresses, use the heavy net which is sold in the drapery, department, or dry-goods stores. The best grade is strong and does not stretch.

To correct round shoulders fit a tight lining, rather snug, across the back through the shoulders and armhole, rather high and close in front. Stand erect while this is being done. The lining will not be real comfortable to wear at first but if you will continue to wear it you will get used to it and get accustomed to an erect position.

GLOSSARY

Accordian Plaiting, laid in plaits, like the bellows of an accordian, by machinery, then steamed and dried to retain this position.

Ajour (a zhur), an aperature made by joining two pieces together.

Albatross (al ba tross), a fine wool material.

Albert Cloth, each side of a different color.

Allover, design extending over entire material.

Antique (an tek), ancient style.

Applique (a ple ka), a separate design applied to the garment it is to adorn.

Apron (a pron), outside garment to protect dress.

Arabesque (ar a besk), an outlined ornamentation in cords, stitchery, or applied pieces.

Armure (ar mur), a fancy weave with small raised design.

Astrakhan (as tra kan), a long pile, closely curled surface to represent the fur of the Astrakhan goat.

Basket weave, woven as a basket weave.

Basque (bask), a tight-fitting waist which extends below the waistline, worn by Basque peasants of France.

Batiste (ba test), a cotton material slightly heavier than lawn; French word for lawn.

Batting, cotton or wool prepared in sheets for interlining.

Bayadere (ba ya der), a material having stripes running from selvage to selvage.

Beaver (be ver), a thick woolen cloth tne wrong side of which is finished with soft, thick nap.

Bedford Cord, a closely woven material having a corded surface, used for women's wear.

Beige (beg), an undyed wool.

Bengaline, a plain, round corded weave, covered with silk or wool.

Bertha, a ruffle, or cape.

Bias, goods cut on long side of a right-angled triangle.

Bishop Sleeve, used in a bishop's robe, and thus named.

Blind-stitch, a stitch not showing.

Blouse, a loose waist dropping over the belt.

Bobbinet, an open lace.

Bodice, a tight-fitting waist or girdle.

Bolero (bo le ro), a Spanish jacket.

Border, trimming usually on edge of material.

Boucle (boo cl), a woolen material with little tufts on surface.

Bouffant (boo fant), full of puffy effect.

Bourette (boo ret), a material on which appears rough threads.

Bradenburg, a fastening for military jacket.

Bretelle, a sort of cape.

Brilliantine, a mohair with glossy surface.

Broadcloth, a fine, glossy woolen.

Brocatelles (bro ka tels), a coarse fabric of silk or wool with figured design.

Broche (bro sha), brocade which has an embroidery effect.

Brussels New, a plain net made first in Brussels but now made in other countries.

Buckram, a coarse material, linen or cotton used for stiffening.

Buckskin, soft as dogskin with more defined twill.

Butcher's Linen, a plain fabric of linen used for dress purposes.

Cabochous (ca bo shous), a jet, glass, steel, or pearl ornament used in dress or millinery.

Cambric, a fabric used for lining in linen or cotton.

Camel's Hair, a fabric made from the hair of the camel or goat, soft and silky.

Canton Flannel, a twilled fabric with nap on one or both sides, used for interlinings of coats and for underwear.

Canvas, a coarse-threaded cotton or linen fabric used for stiffening in collars, cuffs, and coat fronts.

Challis (shally), a soft woolen or woolen and silk fabric.

Chambray (sham bra), a fine, soft cotton material.

Champagne (sham pan), ecru with golden tint.

Chantilly (shan te ye), a town in France once noted for the manufacture of lace.

Chenille (she nel), a thick velvety, corded material of silk or worsted.

Cheviot (chev i ut), a material of the cheviot wool woven diagonally.

Chic (shek), smart style.

Chiffon (shif fon), a thin soft silk material usually crêpe-like in appearance.

Chiffon Velour, velvets of the lightest and softest kind.

Corduroy, a material woven in ribs with pile like velvet, usually of cotton.

Corselet (korslet), body dress.

Cravat, a neck-cloth.

Crêpe (krap), a fabric made of raw silk with crinkled appearance.

Crêpe de Chine (krap de shen), a crimped fabric, made of raw silk, with soft finish.

Cretonne (kre ton), a cotton material with large floral designs.

Damask, to decorate with flowers and rich designs in the weaving.

Decolette (day col tay), gown cut low in neck.

Denim, a coarse, cotton drilling of uncertain origin.

Dimity, a stout, cotton corded fabric.

Doeskin, a firm woolen cloth with a firm soft surface.

Drapelles, very light clothes.

Drilling, a heavy, twilled fabric of linen or cotton.

Drop Skirt, an underskirt, used in place of lining.

Duchesse (duch es), a twilled satin fabric with smooth surface.

Ecru (e cru), a color unbleached in linen, cotton, or silk.

Empiecement, a piece set in.

Empire, fashionable dress during reign of Napoleon I, taken from Greek costumes.

Eolienne, a fabric made of silk or wool, very sheer.

Epaulette (ep pau let), military shoulder trimming.

Esprit, the same as Point d'Spree, a singled or clustered dotted bobbinet. (Esprit means a spirit).

Eton, a short sleeveless jacket.

Eyelet, a round hole worked in garment for lacing.

Faconné (fa son nay), ornamental.

Faille (fal) or (fa y), a soft silk.

Farmers' Satin, a cotton lining of high luster.

Festooned, a draping in curves.

Fichu (fe shoo), a three-cornered piece thrown across the shoulders crossing and draping in front.

Filet (fi lay), a square mesh net.

Flannel, a soft-textured cloth with light nap.

Flannelet, a soft material resembling flannel used for underwear.

Foulard (Fu lard), twilled soft silk.

French Gathers, one short and one long stitch.

Fringe, beads, chenille, or heavy silk or wool threads fastened to a narrow band.

Frogs, ornamental braid-fastenings for coat.

Gaberdine (gab ar den), a coarse frock or loose upper garment formerly worn by Jews. (Webster).

Galatea, a lustrous, strong heavy material of cotton.

Gauntlet Cuff, one flaring at top.

Georgette Crêpe, a sheer crêpe-like silk.

Gigo (jig o), mutton-leg sleeve.

Gingham, a fabric woven in checks or stripes nearly alike on both sides.

Girdle, fitted belt at waist.

Glace, a thin, shiny silk.

Grosgrain (gro grain), a stout double-corded silk with luster.

Gros Jersey (gro Jersey), a textile fabric of heavy quality and close weave.

Guimpe (gimp), yoke and sleeves attached to an underbody, worn with a sleeveless low-necked dress.

Guipure, corded silk trim.

Habit, a skirt without plaits, plain across the back.

Habutai, a Japanese silk.

Homespun, cloth woven by hand or an imitation of such cloth.

Honoton Lace, made by stitching braid upon lace.

Illusion, a plain delicate lace, used for dresses, scarfs, veils, etc.

Jabot (zha bo), or (jab o), neck ornament.

Jupe Cloche or Jupe Tonneau, a cloth, especially for auto riding.

Khaki (kak ke), a tan cloth of cotton used especially in army wear.

Landsdowne, a very beautiful silk and wool material.

Lapel, the revere of a garment.

La Petite, small.

Lawn, a very fine linen or cotton fabric with an open texture, the same as used in the sleeves of a bishop's gown.

Liberty Crêpe, soft crêpe material.

Lingerie (lȯng żhe re), garments made of sheer material.

Maline, a soft gauzy silk.

Marabou, soft down.

Medallion, a design of lace appliqued to a garment.

Melton, thick, smooth woolen cloth used for tailored garments.

Mercerized, a chemical process of hardening the threads to produce a shiny effect.

Meroir, the glossy effect from ironing silk.

Messaline, soft dress silk fabric.

Modiste, a fashionable dressmaker.

Mohair, a fabric made from the hair of the Angora goat; a glossy material.

Moire (mwa re) or (mwar), a watered silk.

Motif, a design in lace, beads, or embroidery.

Mouseline de Soire, a silk muslin, fine and soft.

Negligee (neg li zha), an easy unceremonious attire.

Organdie, a thin transparent cotton.

Oriental Lace, an elegant lace made on a schiffle machine.

Ottaman, a heavy, corded silk usually used for wraps and coats.

Oxford, a wool fabric in dark gray mixtures.

Pagoda, a Grecian sleeve.

Panel, a narrow lengthwise piece of material used in princess dresses and skirts.

Panne (pan), long nap velvet, pressed down and extremely lustrous.

Pannier, side draperies.

Passe (pas sa), out of style and date.

Passementerie, beaded trimming.

Pastel Shades, soft colorings.

Peplum, a short flary skirt or flounce on bottom of waist.

Persian Lamb, fur of baby lambs.

Picot (pe co), an ornamental finish for collars and cuffs, machine made.

Pongee, silk in natural color.

Poplin, a good wearing silk, combined with woolen, linen, or cotton.

Postillion, a kind of basque.

Raglan, a large coat, formerly worn by Lord Raglan of England.

Reding-gote, an outside garment or polonaise opened down the front.

Rep, a corded weave extending crosswise.

Revere, lapel.

Ruche, a strip of material gathered in the center or on the edge and fastened to a band.

Sateen, a lustrous, soft cotton material.

Selesia, a closely woven, fine lining material.

Selvage, edge of material, finished.

Serge, a material in wool woven diagonally.

Shantung, a heavy pongee silk of natural colors.

Silkaline, a mercerized cloth, light weight.

Stole, ornamental material worn each side of front.

Suede (swade), undressed leather.

Sylvette (sil vet), sport cloth.

Taffeta, a light-weight silk alike on both sides.

Taillurs (ta lurs), frock with matching coat.

Tailored, without frills or furbelows, plain in outline.

Tap, a mass of tow ready to put on a distaff.
Taupe (top), dark gray.
Torchon, a bobbinet lace of simple pattern.
Tricot (tre ko), a soft slightly ribbed cloth.
Tunic, an overcoat.
Valenciennes (va len si enz), a narrow edging of lace.
Valour (ve lur), similar to plush, French for velvet.
Velveteen, velvet in cotton.
Venetian, a wool material with twilled surface.
Voile (vwal), a loosely woven material in silk, wool, and cotton.
Volant, a ruffle.
Warp, lengthwise thread of material.
Woof, crosswise or filling thread.
Worsted, twisted thread spun from woolen.
Zephyr, called zephyr gingham, silky appearance with warp coarser than woof.
Zibeline, a hairy wool material.

COURSE OF STUDY

FOR

EVENING DRESSMAKING CLASS

FIRST MONTH

FIRST WEEK:

Lesson I. Organization and Lecture, attendance, punctuality, and advancement.

Lesson II. Materials.

Lesson III. Nap, demonstration and lecture.

Lesson IV. Right side of material, individual instruction.

SECOND WEEK:

Lesson V. Suitable material for extreme figures, demonstration and lecture.

Lesson VI. Shrinking materials, demonstration and individual instruction.

Lesson VII. Demonstration of bad effects of making up materials without shrinking.

Lesson VIII. Review.

THIRD WEEK:

Lesson IX. Taking measures, demonstration and individual instruction.

Lesson X. Taking measures, continued.

Lesson XI. Taking measures, concluded.

Lesson XII. Alteration of patterns, demonstration and lecture.

FOURTH WEEK:

Lesson XIII. Alteration of patterns for extreme figures, demonstration and individual instruction.

Lesson XIV. Alteration of sleeve pattern, demonstration and individual instruction (changing two-piece coat sleeve pattern to a bishop sleeve).

Lesson XV. Cutting and shaping cuffs, demonstration and individual instruction.

Lesson XVI. Questions.

SECOND MONTH

FIRST WEEK:

Lesson XVII. Alteration of waist patterns, designing and cutting collars, demonstration and individual instruction.

Lesson XVIII. Alteration of skirt patterns.

Lesson XIX. Alteration of skirt patterns, continued, cutting yokes, circular skirts, circular bands, circular flounces from seven gore foundation.

Lesson XX. Making a plaited skirt from a seven gore foundation, lecture, questions.

SECOND WEEK:

Lesson XXI. How to add length to a skirt, and how to enlarge a skirt, demonstration and individual instruction.

Lesson XXII. To change style of pattern, demonstration and lecture.

Lesson XXIII. Style of pattern for different figures, demonstration and individual instruction.

Lesson XXIV. Examination.

THIRD WEEK:

Lesson XXV. Equipment, the necessity of, with object lesson.

Lesson XXVI. Dress form, making lining and individual instruction.

Lesson XXVII. Lining making, continued.

Lesson XXVIII. Lining making, concluded.

FOURTH WEEK:

Lesson XXIX. Pinning before basting, demonstration showing how to keep one side of seam from puckering.

Lesson XXX. Material required for a garment, demonstration and lecture.

Lesson XXXI. Amount of material, demonstration and individual instruction.

Lesson XXXII. Review.

THIRD MONTH

FIRST WEEK:

Lesson XXXIII. Lecture on thoroughness and care (being thoroughly competent means that you are master and have no reason to worry over your work).

Lesson XXXIV. Fitting a skirt, demonstration and lecture.

Lesson XXXV. Basting and review on pinning, individual instruction.

Lesson XXXVI. Questions.

SECOND WEEK:

Lesson XXXVII. To prevent twisting of two piece sleeve, demonstration.

Lesson XXXVIII. Basting velvets and silks, lecture and demonstration.

Lesson XXXIX. Diagonal basting and padding stitch, demonstration, and individual instruction.

Lesson XL. Review.

THIRD WEEK:

Lesson XLI. Running-stitch, back-stitch, combination-stitch, individual instruction.

Lesson XLII. Tailors' fell-stitch and over-casting, individual instruction.

Lesson XLIII. Tailors' tacks, overhanding, individual instruction.

Lesson XLIV. Questions.

FOURTH WEEK:

Lesson XLV. French seam and hemming, individual instruction.

Lesson XLVI. Cat-stitch or catch-stitch, feather-stitch, individual instruction.

Lesson XLVII. Fagoting, individual instruction.

Lesson XLVIII. Examination.

FOURTH MONTH

FIRST WEEK:

Lesson XLIX. Buttonhole, lecture, their purposes, ornamental and necessary.

Lesson L. Buttonhole and buttonhole-stitch, demonstration and individual instruction.

Lesson LI. Buttonhole and buttonhole-stitch, concluded.

Lesson LII. Tailors' buttonhole and stitch, demonstration and individual instruction. Working over cord.

Second Week:

Lesson LIII. Tailors' buttonhole, concluded.

Lesson LIV. Eyelets and loops, demonstration and individual instruction.

Lesson LV. Eyelets and loops, concluded.

Lesson LVI. Review.

Third Week:

Lesson LVII. French knots, demonstration and individual instruction.

Lesson LVIII. Sewing on buttons, demonstration and individual instruction.

Lesson LIX. Covering button molds, demonstration and individual instruction.

Lesson LX. Review.

Fourth Week:

Lesson LXI. Smocking and marking material for smocking.

Lesson LXII. Smocking, continued.

Lesson LXIII. Smocking, concluded.

Lesson LXIV. Questions.

FIFTH MONTH

FIRST WEEK:

Lesson LXV. Beads, three methods of sewing on, individual instruction.

Lesson LXVI. Tailors' pockets, finished by drawing facing through, and individual instruction.

Lesson LXVII. Pockets, continued and questions.

Lesson LXVIII. Pockets, with lap turned down, individual instruction.

SECOND WEEK:

Lesson LXIX. Small pockets, like vest pocket with lap turned up, demonstration and individual instruction.

Lesson LXX. Pockets, continued.

Lesson LXXI. Pockets, concluded.

Lesson LXXII. Examination.

THIRD WEEK:

Lesson LXXIII. Bound buttonholes, demonstration and individual instruction.

Lesson LXXIV. Patch pockets, demonstration and individual instruction.

Lesson LXXV. Crow-foot, demonstration and individual instruction.

Lesson LXXVI. Crow-foot, concluded.

Fourth Week:

Lesson LXXVII. Arrow-head, demonstration and individual instruction.

Lesson LXXVIII. Continuous placket, demonstration and individual instruction.

Lesson LXXIX. Continuous placket, concluded.

Lesson LXXX. Questions.

SIXTH MONTH

First Week:

Lesson LXXXI. Tailors' plackets, demonstration and individual instruction.

Lesson LXXXII. Tailors' plackets, continued.

Lesson LXXXIII. Tailors' plackets, concluded.

Lesson LXXXIV. Review.

Second Week:

Lesson LXXXV. Cutting bias and shirring bias bands, demonstration and individual instruction.

Lesson LXXXVI. Shirring bias bands, concluded.

Lesson LXXXVII. Bias bands, demonstration and individual instruction.

Lesson LXXXVIII. Bias bands, concluded.

THIRD WEEK:

Lesson LXXXIX. Bias and crosswise straps, demonstration and individual instruction.

Lesson XC. Milliners' folds, demonstration and individual instruction.

Lesson XCI. Bands, straps, and folds, concluded.

Lesson XCII. Questions.

FOURTH WEEK:

Lesson XCIII. Couching, demonstration by hand and machine.

Lesson XCIV. Covering cord, demonstration and individual instruction.

Lesson XCV. Shirring over cord, demonstration and individual instruction.

Lesson XCVI. Examination.

SEVENTH MONTH

FIRST WEEK:

Lesson XCVII. Marking for sewing on hooks and eyes, demonstration and individual instruction.

Lesson XCVIII. Circular yokes, demonstration and individual instruction.

Lesson XCIX. Circular yokes, continued.

Lesson C. Circular yokes, concluded.

SECOND WEEK:

Lesson CI. Making a tight fitting (lace or net) yoke with high fitted collar attached to fitted lining, demonstration and individual instruction.

Lesson CII. Lesson CI. continued.

Lesson CIII. Lesson CI. concluded.

Lesson CIV. Review.

THIRD WEEK:

Lesson CV. Tucking circular skirts, demonstration and individual instruction.

Lesson CVI. Tucking circular skirts concluded.

Lesson CVII. Review, fitting a skirt, demonstration and lecture.

Lesson CVIII. Finishing top of skirt, demonstration and lecture. Questions.

FOURTH WEEK:

Lesson CIX. Getting the length of a skirt, demonstration and lecture on position and use of skirt ruler.

Lesson CX. Putting the hem in a skirt and basting in sleeve, demonstration and individual instruction.

Lesson CXI. Bound open welt seam and strap seam, demonstration and individual instruction.

Lesson CXII. Questions.

EIGHTH MONTH

FIRST WEEK:

Lesson CXIII. Imitation strap seam and slot seam, demonstration and individual instruction.

Lesson CXIV. Raw edge lap seam and fell seam, demonstration, and individual instruction.

Lesson CXV. Review.

Lesson CXVI. Matching flowers and stripes and matching plaids, demonstration and individual instruction. Questions.

SECOND WEEK:

Lesson CXVII. Cutting a garment so as to not have two pieces for one side, and length of girl's skirts for different ages, lecture.

Lesson CXVIII. Pressing and to take shine off, demonstration and individual instruction.

Lesson CXIX. Finishing the top of skirt, lecture.

Lesson CXX. Examination.

THIRD WEEK:

Lesson CXXI. Lines, lecture and class to discuss lines.

Lesson CXXII. Combining colors, lecture.

Lesson CXXIII. Putting canvas in front of coat, demonstration, and individual instruction.

Lesson CXXIV. Putting tape in front of coat, demonstration and individual instruction.

Fourth Week:

Lesson CXXV. Review of Lesson CXXIII.

Lesson CXXVI. Review of Lesson CXXIV.

Lesson CXXVII. Questions.

Lesson CXXVIII. Review.

NINTH MONTH

First Week:

Lesson CXXIX. Study of Glossary.

Lesson CXXX. Miscellaneous.

Lesson CXXXI. Study of Glossary.

Lesson CXXXII. Miscellaneous.

Second Week:

Lesson CXXXIII. Study of Glossary.

Lesson CXXXIV. Miscellaneous.

Lesson CXXXV. Review.

Lesson CXXXVI. Questions.

Third Week:

Lesson CXXXVII. Study of Glossary.

Lesson CXXXVIII. Miscellaneous.

Lesson CXXXIX. Review.
Lesson CXL. Questions.

Fourth Week:

Lesson CXLI. Study of Glossary.
Lesson CXLII. Miscellaneous.
Lesson CXLIII. Examination.
Lesson CXLIV. Closing.

Lightning Source UK Ltd.
Milton Keynes UK
UKHW022323021120
372685UK00003B/209

9 781359 416063